PRAISE FOR AIM FOR THE MIDDLE FROM AI

M.K. Jackson humorously tackles the self-help genre by promoting the idea of achieving happiness, success, and love through embracing mediocrity.

CHATGPT

Jackson's work is a delightful parody of the self-help industry. The tongue-in-cheek advice to aim for mediocrity is refreshing and liberating.

CHATGPT

The funniest parts are Jackson's candid confessions and the playful dismantling of self-help clichés. His irreverent tone and witty analogies make the book an entertaining read, reminding us not to take life too seriously and to find joy in the middle ground.

CHATGPT

This humorous take on common self-help practices, like goal setting and journaling, exposes the often absurd lengths people go to in the pursuit of success and happiness.

CHATGPT

Jackson introduces the idea that mediocrity is humanity's default state and should be embraced rather than shunned... liberating readers from the pressure of over-achievement.

CHATGPT

If you're tired of self-help books that demand too much, Jackson's "Aim for the Middle" is the perfect antidote.

CHATGPT

AIM FOR THE MIDDLE

HOW TO ACHIEVE HAPPINESS, SUCCESS, AND
LOVE THROUGH THE UNBRIDLED POWER OF
MEDIOCRITY

M.K. JACKSON

Purple Prose Publishing LLC

Published by Purple Prose Publishing LLC

Los Angeles, California 90042

info@purpleprosepublishing.com

www.purpleprosepublishing.com

Published 2024

ISBN: 979-8-9851041-1-0 (paperback)

ISBN: 979-8-9851041-0-3 (ebook)

Library of Congress Control Number: 2024912447

DISCLAIMER

CONTENTS

PART THREE
THE FIVE PILLARS OF AN ADEQUATE LIFE

For Eleanor

If you're looking for self-help, why would you read a book written by somebody else? That's not self-help, that's help. There is no such thing as self-help. If you did it yourself, you didn't need help.

—George Carlin

PREFACE

In a recent Gallup poll, only fifty percent of respondents described themselves as "completely satisfied" with their current job. In the same poll, a paltry thirty-two percent reported being "completely satisfied" with the amount of money they earn.[1]

A survey conducted by NORC at the University of Chicago found that only fourteen percent of American adults consider themselves "very happy."[2]

According to Cigna's Loneliness Index (I can't even imagine how depressing it must be to work in that office), a survey of more than 20,000 United States adults ages eighteen years and older revealed forty-six percent are either "sometimes" or "always" lonely. And just fifty-three percent of the respondents have "meaningful in-person social interactions, such as having an extended conversation with a friend or spending quality time with family, on a daily basis."

The self-help industrial complex is an $11 billion industry and you need only consider the previous statistics to know why.[3] Self-diagnosed unsuccessful, unhappy, and unloved people spend a lot of money to de-"un" themselves into successful, happy, and loved people. The process is often long, expensive, and a lot of effort. (I'm exhausted just typing it.).

But there's something even more concerning. The vast majority of these programs, classes, books, videos, podcasts, seminars, and webinars begin with the central premise that the person is *not* already successful, happy, or loved. Thus begins the arduous pedal-to-the-metal process of whipping up a lifeus maximus from scratch to replace the one that already existed in the first place. And *that's* the subtle yet radical difference between the self-help industrial complex and this book: I believe we're all born successful, happy, and loved. The problem is we just don't always know it. Success, happiness, and love are not conditions or situations that must be installed in us by some external mechanism—especially ones that are laborious, expensive, and cut into our crucial video streaming time. The cruel irony is that the only thing preventing our success, happiness, and love is our own inability to realize it's already ours by birthright. Why we do that and how to remedy it is why I wrote this book.

I'm M.K. Jackson, MFA (more on that title in a moment). I possess no degrees, credentials, or certifications in psychology, sociology, anthropology, or any other behavioral science for that matter. I've never read a psychology textbook, worked in social services, or counseled anyone on anything. I've never even successfully negotiated a lower cable bill. So, what qualifies me to tell you how to be successful, happy, and loving? In a word, *disillusionment*.

Having listened to countless audiobooks, videos, and webinars (reading just seemed like too much to ask of myself), I've experienced first-hand the ineffectual pursuit of success, happiness, and love through the self-help industrial complex. This many habits, that many agreements, these prophecies, those secrets, unleash this, let go of that. Yet I remained unmoved, unmotivated, and unimproved. Why? Because every one of those books, courses, programs, videos, audios, seminars, webinars, strategies, technologies, and cult of personalities have one thing in common: they're a metric shit-ton of work. I mean you *really* have to bust your ass if you want results (and baby, my ass has already been busted enough).

I totally understand why there are so many fucked-up people in the world considering the endless goal setting, vision boarding, and journaling required to de-fuck yourself. I just don't have it in me to try that hard anymore. (Something about threshold and motivation if I remember correctly.) And it's not because I'm lazy or a quitter. To the contrary, from completing the entire twenty miles on my first March of Dimes Walk-a-Thon when I was eleven years old, to finishing this book nearly five decades later, *I don't quit.*

I don't try too hard either.

You know that school report card thing "does not apply himself?" That's mine. I invented that. I am profoundly gifted at not trying too hard—in everything. It's my wheelhouse, my expertise, my art, my religion. I carried a consistent, bulletproof C+ average from grade school to high school, into college, and through graduate school. It was like watching an electrocardiogram flatline for fifty years straight. Not a goddamn blip. Just a five-decade-long *beeeeeeeeeeeeeeeeeep.*

Yet I "earned" two academic degrees in my life—TWO! A Bachelor of Arts in my twenties, and a Master of Fine Arts in my fifties. But it's no accident that both degrees have the word *arts* in them. Given the arts are so much easier than the sciences or the businesses, I chose degrees that used coloring books rather than textbooks. I didn't quit... but I didn't try too hard either.

After I finished graduate school, while looking at my diploma and marveling at the fact that I had once again pulled one over on academia, I was suddenly imbued with a divine revelation: even though I invested only the ~~most~~ least minimal C-average effort in my MFA studies, I still "earned" the exact same degree as the A+ student who worked ten times harder than I did. They don't print your GPA on the diploma so no one will ever know who got As and who got Cs. The only difference between that over-achieving show-off's diploma and mine is the name below "conferred upon." At the end of the day we both have the same useless MFA and the same opportunity not to gain employment with it. It turns out that whole *work hard and you'll achieve your dreams* thing is inconsistent with the facts—at least in my case... and I'm willing to bet in yours as well.

This realization excited me. I wanted that same minimal effort success (and, subsequently, happiness) I enjoyed in my *academic* life throughout my *real* life as well. My previous research found no significant correlation between *greater effort* and *better results*. Meaning, that just working hard for something does *not* in and of itself guarantee success. In fact, one can work *too hard* for something and the value of what is accomplished does not justify the expenditure of time and effort it took to obtain it. Conversely, there are also instances when one attains exactly what they desire with relatively little endeavor, thus serving up that old chestnut *if you can dream it you can achieve it* on a silver platitude.

I figured there must be hundreds, if not dozens of people in the world who, like me, yearn for a *minimal commitment/moderate results* brand of self-improvement. Building upon my own underwhelming life as the basis for a loosely structured plan, I sifted through lots of statistics I had no way of understanding, theories I had no interest in comprehending, and affirmations I had no intention of affirming. The data solidified what I already knew: I'm simply not willing to work that hard for something I'm not sure is worth the effort.

But what about other people? What have they learned about success, happiness, and love that could be edifying? I needed to talk to folks at a place in their lives where the power of their failures had crushed their hope to such an intensity that their regret would be instructive. So, I interviewed embittered people on their deathbeds. And unsurprisingly they all said pretty much the same three things to me:

1. "Who are you?"
2. "What're you in my hospital room?" and
3. "Are you here to finally clean my bedpan?"

What I learned is that the golden years aren't so golden when you're dumping bedpan after bedpan filled with piss and shit into a hospital room garbage can—especially for uncooperative, remarkably belligerent people in the ICU who really should've been more thankful that anyone was showing interest in them and their shit and piss filled bedpans.

Oh well. Back to the drawing board.

I decided to change my approach. Maybe looking to others for their assessment of success, happiness, and love was the wrong tact as the bedpans had so incontestably attested. Maybe I needed to look closer to home. Maybe I needed to look to myself.

As with any universal human truth free of institutional bias and unreasonable effort, the *authentic* answers are found deep within ourselves. Only through soul searching, personal reflection, and the courage to face our demons, can we attain profound and everlasting success, happiness, and love.

Yeah, I guess so, but fuck. It all still seemed like a lotta work. Shit like journaling and goal setting and getting up early in the morning. All that twaddle the self-help industrial complex mongers. The same bunkum I'm trying to avoid.

Again, back to the drawing board.

Eventually, my process of ducking, diverting, and deferring coalesced into a radical rethinking of success, happiness, and love. They became less tangible. No longer extrinsic, ephemeral *things* to attain, but enduring, transcendental states to discover. In other words, "yes," true *anything* comes from within.

I liked that. I worked for me. Well, except that I couldn't do it.

If success, happiness, and love were indeed within, I sure didn't hear them calling out to me above the din of trying too hard, setting goals, and changing bedpans. But attaining success, happiness, and love is not working hard to become some*thing*. It's cutting through the clutter and calming the chaos to discover the some*one* you already are.

Regardless of the trite bromides other people and institutions flog to define success, happiness, and love to *their* agendas (instead of *yours*), not everyone achieves at the same level, produces at the same quantity, or is cut out for the same greatness. And that's okay—especially since those metrics really have nothing to do with true success, happiness, and love.

If you are unsuccessful, unhappy, and unloved, it's because you're trying too hard. But if you're willing to lower your sights and aim for the middle, you'll be astounded at what adequacy can do for you.

In my case, I simply embraced *good enough*, turned it into *just enough*, and made it *more than enough*. Now, in this book, I'm going to show you how to do the same.

M.K. Jackson
Los Angeles, 2024

INTRODUCTION

Congratulations! You've made it this far in the book! Such commitment this early on definitely means you're serious about increasing the quality of your life through the unbridled power of mediocrity.

Countless people spend their entire lives looking for the meanings of success, happiness, and love. Me? I just looked in the dictionary and there they were...

success (noun): the achieving of the results wanted or hoped for; something that achieves positive results.

happy (adjective): feeling, showing, or causing pleasure or satisfaction.

love (verb): to like another adult very much and be romantically and sexually attracted to them, or to have strong feelings of liking a friend or person in your family.

Unfortunately, the *Cambridge Dictionary* is a bit vague on how they can be attained for purposes of life fulfillment.

Not to worry. You can also look for success, happiness, and love on Amazon (the dot-com, not the rainforest). As of this writing, an Amazon Books search for *success* returns over 60,000 results, *happiness* also nets over 60,000, and a query for *love* gets you over 70,000. Obviously they're all very popular topics. (By contrast, search *eating vegetables*, and you get a comparatively minuscule 10,000 returns.) However, while most of the books and their authors do indeed connect the dots between success, happiness, and love and an awesome, kick-ass new life, there is a devious catch: these books deliver the goods *only* if you exert *maximum effort*—and that means working hard. Really hard. You'd think reading an entire book would be asking enough of a person, but these tomes also require goal setting, journaling, workbooking, drafting plans, keeping calendars, taping shit to your bathroom mirror, and waking up early at an ungodly hour to do it all. Really early. Like, goddamned early. Some of these self-help programs even require you to exercise physically.

Fortunately, if you don't like to read, you can listen. There are thousands of audiobooks and podcasts unlocking the doors to success, happiness, and love. But be forewarned of the bait-and-switch here. Just because it's easier to listen than to read, don't think you're off the hook. You still have to get up early to set goals, journal, and accomplish a lot of other ridiculously difficult shit. And I don't mean crap like eating more vegetables or calling your friends more often. I'm talking about inane pursuits like landing your dream job, making a million dollars, and losing weight. Just *one* of those things is a life-long pursuit of never-ending agony and disappointment—but *all three* at once?

Are you a watcher rather than a listener? YouTube has thousands of videos on success, happiness, and love. You *might* find something of value in that digital sludge, but I doubt it. Now that everyone's pocket phone has a movie camera, anyone with half-baked opinions can post a video. That means there's *a lot* of crap out there: unfounded theories, axe grindings, revenue streams, and auditions to become the next big influencer. More often than not, the purpose of these videos is to build the creator's brand, not yours.

Do you prefer more modern tools for success, happiness, and love? You're in luck. There's an app for that—actually, scores of them. Coaching apps, motivational apps, journaling apps, goal-setting apps, and entrepreneurial apps. Apps for planning, apps for scheduling, and apps for accounting. There are even apps for making apps. Trouble achieving a happy balance between your personal and professional life? No problem. There are health apps, fitness apps, lifestyle apps, affirmation apps, and calming apps. Apps with relaxers, mood trackers, and white noise makers. Wellness apps, mindfulness apps, meditation apps, and even breathing apps (in case you don't know how to breathe). Maybe you're looking for love (or the next best thing for an hour or two). Finding that perfect someone has never been easier. With the right app, you can custom order a soulmate just like you would a pizza. There are dating apps, hookup apps, adultery apps, apps for young love, apps for old love, and apps for middle love. Straight apps, gay apps, bisexual apps, transgender apps, asexual apps. And if things don't work out between you and your cybermate, don't sweat it. You can start all over again with a divorce app.

With all this information and advice out there readily accessible by reading, listening, watching, and swiping, you'd think finding success, happiness, and love in the twenty-first century would be a snap (or a tap). But it seems the more books, blogs, podcasts, programs, seminars, webinars, videos, and apps, the wider, deeper, and colder the chasm between us and our success, happiness, and love becomes.

Because you're reading this book, it's my assertion (and you know what they say when you make an assertion: *you make an ass insertion*), that you've tried other methods, courses, and schemes for success, happiness, and love, and came up short. That's completely understandable for all the reasons I listed in the preface. (*What??? You didn't read the preface? Why is it most readers skip over the preface? Seriously, there's important info in the preface. If you didn't read it, please go back and do so. Thanks, MKJ.*) But if your "journey" into self-improvement has you searching for an easier pathway to success, happiness, and love, one of minimal effort for commensurate results, you've come to the right place.

So, what does this book have that other books don't? Actually, it's what those other books have that this one *doesn't*: hard work. This book gives the boot *and* the finger to all those ineffectual cornerstones of the self-help industrial complex including journaling, goal setting, affirmations, and worst of all, waking up extra early in the morning just to journal, set goals, and affirm.

Within these pages, you'll discover...

The Mediocrity Principle. Scientific evidence that mediocre performance is humanity's default and your cosmic birthright. Imagine how amazing you'll feel once the oppressive weight of overachievement is finally lifted from your shoulders.

The 5 or 6 Destructive Beliefs Preventing You from Achieving Success, Happiness, and Love. Subconscious, self-sabotaging thinking, like *Try harder... Dream bigger...* and *You can do anything you put your mind to.* Minacious notions that waste your valuable time while setting you up for ultimate failure.

The Five Pillars of an Adequate Life. EZ-to-understand, even EZer-to-master principles for a more realistically attainable life of success, happiness, and love, built on a foundation of not quitting... but not trying too hard either. With these pillars, you'll understand the complete folly in chasing that cryptozoological creature known as "the perfect life." It's exhausting, excruciating, and pointless.

And there's more—*much more!*

Aim for the Middle is your wake-up call with a snooze button. If you're willing to do less than it takes to create a life that's good enough, you'll achieve dreams below your wildest expectations. So c'mon—give it a shot. What've you got to lose? I mean, you already bought the book.

You have a rendezvous with mediocrity!

HOW TO USE THIS BOOK

I never really understood this section of how-to books. But most have one, so I figured I better include one in mine too.

How to use this book? How do you use a fork? How do you use a doorknob? Need to know how to use a shirt?

Books are pretty self-explanatory. I mean they've been around for like, two thousand years. They have a very intuitive interface: read a page, turn it, read the next page. There isn't any required programming like with your phone answering machine or VCR. You don't have to buy the vowels like on *Wheel of Fortune* because they come free with the text. And since books are already assembled for you there are no IKEA-like erection catastrophes with oversimplified instructions, diagrams, missing parts, or lost Allen wrenches. Hell, the pages are even sequentially numbered so there's no danger you'll read them out of order.

How to use this book? Just start on the first page and keep reading until it's over.

WARNING! EFFORT ALERT!

This book contains assignments that involve thinking and writing on the part of you, the reader.

Procurement of writing instruments (pencil/pen and paper) will be required. A modicum of time and energy on your part will be requested.

Now, you're probably thinking: *what the hell is this bullshit? This book is supposed to be about being successful, happy, and in love **through the unbridled power of mediocrity**—along with the advertised promise of not trying too hard. That, by its very definition, means **with the least amount of effort possible**.*

Yes, that's true.

And it's still true.

The exercises in this book have been designed to be brief, painless, and require **much less** effort than assignments and activities requisite in all those other books paying tongue service to the self-help industrial complex.

In fact, the assignments in this book require so much less of you—less work, less time, less trying—I'm not even calling them exercises, I'm calling them *LESSercises*.

Therefore, before we begin, I must establish a few ground rules to ensure these lessercises produce the maximum benefit from the most minimal effort humanly possible:

1. You must use a *single* piece of paper for each lessercise.

Not a notebook, not a journal, not a diary. I cannot stress this enough for the following reasons:

- if there are other pieces of paper available, you might be inclined to utilize them, increasing the amount of work you do and we can have none of that nonsense;
- by writing on multiple pieces of paper bound within a single volume, the lessercise would dangerously approach *journaling*, which is far too much effort than is necessary or required and we can have none of that nonsense, either.

2. Do not use a computer for the lessercises.

Some of you might be inclined to break out your computer, fire up Evernote, Excel, Trello, Lucidchart, Smartsheet, or some other unnecessarily complicated software so you can organize, strategize, formulize, Kanban, image map, and Gantt chart your lessercises in fancy grid patterns with extraneous text headers saved to a folder placed in a folder and nested within another folder in an overly complicated hierarchical organization of failed simplicity.

This is a surefire indication that you possess the destructive tendency to overachieve. ***Resist this temptation!*** The net results from this extra effort will not provide greater insights, clearer pathways, or more effectual solutions than if you simply draw it out on paper. If you can handwrite it in five seconds, why the hell would you take a half hour to do it on a computer? Who are you trying to impress?

3. Do NOT overthink the lessercises—*Overthinking is overrated*^{TM}.

Brain power burns *a lot* of fuel. Sometimes even more than physical work. When asked to answer questions in a lessercise:

- write the first answer that pops into your head. If nothing pops;
- grab an answer that's already floating around in your brain. You've been present for pretty much your entire life, so you probably have all the answers tucked away somewhere in your melon. Dust off the cobwebs and recycle those answers—it's much easier than thinking of new ones.

Remember: now is *not* the time to rise to the occasion and get all insightful by reflecting on your life. (The time for that has long passed.) We are now in triage mode—possibly even code blue for some of you.

Finally, no matter the level of disdain you may harbor for the lessercises, know that the [minimal] effort you invest now will greatly reduce the pain of future exertion in your pursuit of success, happiness, and love. Think of it like... like... I dunno... I really can't think of an analogy because I no longer try too hard in anything. Oh, I know. Think of these lessercises like that clear coat they put on new cars to save you the time and cost of painting your car later on down the line. No. Wait. That's a bad example. We all know that stuff's a swindle... Okay, I got it: think of the lessercises like a teeth cleaning. The little effort you spend getting your teeth cleaned now saves you the pain and expense down the road of having your teeth pulled out by the roots and wearing dentures for the rest of your life. Yeah, that works.

Now that I've talked you off the ledge, let's get on with the book.

PART ONE
GETTING IT ALL TOGETHER

CHAPTER 1
AIM FOR THE MIDDLE

The middle of the road is all of the usable surface.
—Dwight D. Eisenhower

That's from the guy who was a Five-Star General in the Army, Supreme Commander of the Allied Expeditionary Force in Europe, and President of the United States. If he aimed for the middle, you know I'm onto something.
—M. K. Jackson

In archery, you aim for the middle, because that's where the bullseye is.

To resolve a conflict between two opposing parties, we aim for the middle ground, a place where everyone agrees.

In golf, you increase the odds of a birdie by aiming for the middle of the green.

Between the endeavor for upper-class status and the struggle from lower-class existence lies the content of middle-class bliss.

And after the frustrating failure of inadequate words to communicate passionate animus for a person, place, or thing, comes the immense gratification of simply expressing it with the middle finger.*

The middle is the sweet spot. It's the perfect place to be. The middle is accessible and obtainable, comfortable, and reasonable.

Goldilocks and the Three Levels

Aim too high and you're one of these up-at-dawn, over-achieving, high-impact, 24/7 go-getters who just don't know when to quit. Literally. Aim too low and you're sunk, stuck neck-deep in apathetic atrophy where you don't care about anything and won't care about anyone. But aim for the middle and you'll strike the perfect balance. The harmonious middle is where we find true success, lasting happiness, and consummate love.

High, low, middle. Just like for Goldilocks, one is too hard, one is too soft, and one is juuuuust right. Here's why...

Aiming too High

Flat out NO ONE needs to try this hard. And no one after reading this book better ever try this hard again. At this stratospheric supereminence level, you'll NEVER be successful, happy, or in love because you won't have the goddamn time. You'll be too busy showing off making lists, setting goals, filling journals,

---

* Unless of course, you're in Britain, in which case it would be "two fingers up." Oh shit. I never thought of this until now, but that necessitates a new cover design for the British release of this book. Something I didn't do. Shit. The whole "middle finger" image won't mean shit across the pond. I need a backward peace/victory/fuck off sign. But that doesn't integrate into the title for the logo— I'd need a logo with two fingers. Shit. That means a new *book title* to accommodate *that* design—something like... *Aim for the V*. Shit. That sounds vaguely misogynistic. Besides, if I change the title, it changes the entire metaphorical approach to the subject—so that means a complete rewrite. Shit... How many other countries in the world also don't use the middle finger? Shit, I'll be rewriting this book over and over until I die—like George Lucas with the original *Star Wars* trilogy. What kind of "aiming for the middle" (or for the "V") message would I be sending then? Shit.

and waking up early. You'll be exhausted, suffering from goal fatigue, aspiration asphyxiation, and carpal tunnel syndrome.

Aiming too Low

At this level, you've thrown in the towel. You're in a state of hyper-ennui—a level of complete mental, physical, and emotional lethargy. No interests, no enthusiasm, no escape. Aiming too low you can not be successful, happy, or in love because you've given up on yourself. Down here, you'll have to try a *bit* harder (but not too hard).

Aiming for the Middle

You'll find plenty of free-range success, happiness, and love grazing in the midlands. Aiming for the middle is about *balance*. Not devoting every second of your day to overachieving, nor wasting all your time underachieving, leaves plenty of time in your life for *middleachieving*. That's when your success, happiness, and love are realized not by action items, but through *inaction* items. Things like sleeping, spending time with your family, Netflix binging, spending time with your friends, pursuing things on your *fucket list**, spending time alone, Amazon Prime binging, and taking a nap.

Are You High, Low, or Adequately in the Middle?

Reading those descriptions of the three levels I'm guessing

---

* A fucket list is like a bucket list but way better. It's full of things you want to do before you catch the night train to the big auf wiedersehen, but the shit is so different, so *not* you, so insane, you don't dare put it on your bucket list because of the testicular/ovarian fortitude it takes to do it. But sometimes, there comes a point in life when things are so good—or so bad—doing something completely unhinged and out-of-character is the only way to go so you just say: "Fucket, let's do this shit!"

you could take a pretty good guess where you're currently aiming. And because you're reading this book, I'm guessing I could guess what you're guessing. But this is *your* success, happiness, and love at stake here so there's no room for guessing. If you're truly going to be successful, happy, and loving, you need to know where in the hell you're aiming.

I've taken a rather large chunk of my very valuable personal time to cook up a test for just such a purpose. Based on results from a multivariate statistical analysis I want to conduct using independent data sets in a rotation estimation, I've devised three predictive models for your stratification pleasure. I call this evaluation and classification the *Success & Happiness Indicator Test*™. By taking a SHIT daily you can assess where you are within the three levels and avoid the low and high while maintaining the middle.

The Success and Happiness Indicator Test

If you don't know shit from Crayola, fear not. My SHIT is very easy to take. The SHIT's divided into three levels of applied motivational behavior: aiming too *low*, aiming too *high*, and aiming for the *middle*.

While it's only possible to be on one level at a time, it's not impossible to be on different levels within the same month, week, or even day. Bouncing around between levels is very discombobulating to your internal mediocrity sextant. That's why you *must* monitor this SHIT every day.

The SHIT has three objectives:

1. Identify the level at which you are currently functioning (low, middle, or high).
2. Steer you away from the low and high levels and toward the middle.
3. Using the results to achieve *level singularity* (keeping in the middle).

The best way to illustrate how the test works is for us to take a SHIT together…

WARNING! EFFORT ALERT!
The following section involves thinking and writing. Minimal time and effort on the part of you, the reader, will be required.

To ensure maximum benefit with minimal effort, please remember to follow these three rules:

1. Use a *single* piece of paper for the lessercise—more pages = more work.
2. Do *not* use a computer for the lessercises—embrace analog.
3. Do *not* overthink the lessercises—overthinking is overrated.

SHIT Questions for Behavior Level One: *Aiming Too Low*

Ask yourself these three simple true or false questions. Score 1 point for each true answer and 0 (zero) points for each false answer.

1. *If I run out of milk, rather than taking the trouble to go to the store for more, I just pour water over my breakfast cereal.*
2. *After the first wearing, I turn my underwear inside out and wear them again, so I have less laundry to do.*
3. *I have not read everything in this book up to this point.*

SHIT Questions for Behavior Level Two: *Aiming Too High*

As with the first category, ask yourself the following three

true or false questions. Again, score 1 point for a true answer and
0 (zero) points for a false answer.

1. *I get up at least thirty minutes earlier than necessary in the
   morning to journal and/or set goals.*
2. *When binge-watching a series on a streaming service, at the
   end of an episode I click the "play next" button rather than
   letting it auto-play to the next video.*
3. *People (friends, family, significant other, coworkers, etc.)
   congratulate me on "a job well done" by one or more of the
   following: a verbal thank you, a literal pat on the back, a
   thank you card, a gift card, a pay raise, sex.*

SHIT Questions for Behavior Level Three: *Aiming for the
Middle*

Let's see if you are indeed successfully aiming for the middle
by answering the following true/false statements. You know the
drill—for each true answer score one (1) point; for each false
answer, score zero (0) points.

1. *My first action item for the day is breakfast.*
2. *I perform at my most middlist throughout the day because I
   don't use other people's definitions of success and happiness
   —but I do use a batter dispenser to make pancakes for
   breakfast.*
3. *I hit the sack at night fully rested.*

Scoring Your SHIT

Before I reveal what the score for each level means, take
solace knowing that the majority of people taking their first SHIT
usually end up aiming too high or too low. Truth be told, if

you're new to the strategies and technologies of this book it's highly unlikely your scoring will land you in the middle level since empowerment through mediocrity will probably be new to you. (However, if for some reason you are naturally operating in the middle level don't think for a second you're getting a refund for this book—especially since odds are you purchased it at a substantially marked-down price.)

Now, on with your results…

SHIT Answer Scores for Behavior One: *Aiming Too Low*

0 = Good news! You are *not* aiming too low. Then again, this doesn't mean you're not aiming too high or middling either.

1 = Technically speaking, I wouldn't say that scoring a one between all three questions means you're aiming low. Could be you're just lazy. But keep an eye on it. If this persists, you'll need to get some skin in the game.

2 = Whoa, dude, you're really phoning it in. Like, with a Motorola StarTAC 1996 flip phone. You better do something about your apathy before it's too late.

3 = RED LIGHT should be flashing! RED LIGHT should be flashing!

WARNING! If you scored three on this level, you're *aiming waaaaaaay too low* and you my friend are in deep shit—and I don't mean SHIT like in the *Success & Happiness Indicator Test*™, I mean "shit" as in actual *shit*. Please consider seeking assistance from a qualified professional immediately before you suffer from terminal apathy atrophy.

SHIT Answer Scores for Behavior Two: *Aiming Too High*

0 = Exhale a sigh of relief, you are definitely *not* aiming too high. However, this doesn't necessarily mean you are aiming for the middle. Please ascertain your score in the *Aiming for the Middle* category before initiating any celebratory actions.

1 = Whoa! Hold your horses there, reverse cowgirl. How do you even have time to read this book when you're spending so much time overachieving? The only action you should be taking now is *in*action.

2 = What in the H E double hockey sticks are you trying to prove??? You are dangerously close to falling into the *self-help industrial complex vortex*. And just like a cigarette butt flushed down the toilet, once you're trapped in the overpowering swirl, it'll pull you right down the drainpipes into the sewer.

Before it's too late, take a sick day (or two) from work. Add another video streaming service to your lineup and watch it. Take a nap. Hydrate. But most importantly, DO NOT attempt *any* accomplishments in your current condition. Your perspective is skewed and judgment impaired.

3 = DANGER, WILL ROBINSON! DANGER!

WARNING! Scoring a three in the *Aiming Too High* category places you squarely in the crosshairs of the self-help industrial complex. It's only a matter of time before you are lost in the colossal time sucks of journaling, webinars, and [gulp] GOALS—if you aren't already.

At this level, all we can do is triage and pray that you have not fully surrendered physically, psychologically, and emotionally to this cult of madness. IF you can still hear me... IF the grace of God is still within your grasp... PLEASE, commit at least one, preferably two, of the actions on the *Aiming Too Low* scale to balance this SHIT out before it's too late!

SHIT Answer Scores for Behavior Three: *Aiming for the Middle*

0 = Man, I don't know if you're trying too hard or you're not trying enough. Either way, you're pretty freaking far from the middle. Please reassess by reviewing the questions and applying them as *instructions* for living your life in blissful mediocrity.

1 = Well, I guess doing one is better than doing none...but just barely.

2 = This is an excellent score—You're in a position to build upon your mediocrity and live a happy, successful, loving life.

3 = OUTSTANDING! All indications... indicate that you are squarely on your way to becoming a *master of mediocrity*. BUT you must continue your *commitment to middling* as outlined in this book by not working too hard, underperforming, reigning in your expectations, and *never quitting* but not trying too hard either.

The Perfect SHIT Score

Optimally, when you're firing on all mediocre pistons, your SHIT will score thusly:

Aiming too Low = 0
Aiming too High = 0
Aiming for the Middle = 3

If your score reveals you're aiming too low you *must* aim slightly higher—but not into the extraneous ether where superfluous effort fails to produce commensurate results. If you have no idea what I'm talking about or how to do it, don't freak out. This book will help you. You will learn techniques and acquire tools to keep yourself in the middle where all things are possible —especially success, happiness, and love.

If you scored aiming too high, slow down Kid Dyn-o-mite. You must aim slightly lower, but not too low into the depths of indifference. If you have no idea what I'm talking about or how to do it, don't freak out. This book will help you. You will learn techniques and acquire tools to keep yourself in the middle where all things are possible—especially success, happiness, and love.

And if your score clocks you aiming right in the middle, don't even *think* about asking for your money back on this book because I'm not issuing refunds for any goddamned reason.

Especially because one good SHIT does not a desired life make. Personally, I don't even give *two* SHITS to determine that because konsistency is King. SHITs naturally fluctuate throughout the month, week, or even day so expect to take more than one. You might be middling today, lowballing tomorrow, or highreaching the next day. The trick is to continually keep your SHIT at a 0-0-3 score to maintain congruency. If you have no idea what I'm talking about or how to do it, don't freak out. This book will help you. You will learn techniques and acquire tools to keep yourself consistently in the middle where all things are possible.

And with that, congratulations are in order! You made it through the first chapter. So, are you still on board and willing to go through with this thing? I sure hope so because I'm not issuing refunds for any goddamned reason.

What I *am* issuing is a challenge. I'm challenging you to embrace the not-so-really-tested concepts in this book for a life of success, happiness, and love and not request a refund.

CHAPTER 2
YOUR SUCCESSFUL, HAPPY, LOVING LIFE (PART 1)

It's your life. You don't know how long it's gonna be, but you know it's got a bad ending.
—Don Draper, *Mad Men*, "Six Month Leave" (S2 E9)

I'm pretty sure my life has three *bad endings — like that* Clue *movie.*
—M.K. Jackson

Welcome back. By your presence in this chapter, I gather you've thrown logic to the wind, decided not to request a refund, and are ready and willing to embrace the ideologies in this book. Let's boogie!

Success. Happiness. Love.

Humans have pondered, postulated, and pursued these three separate yet interrelated basic human needs for millennia.

Does success make you happy?

Does being happy make you successful?

Can you be happy without success?

Can you be happy with success?

Can you be successful in love?

Does love make you happy?

Does happiness make you successful in love?

Can you be a happy, unsuccessful person if you're in love with an unhappy successful person?

And could you ever have a successful relationship with a happy person who's in love with you while you're unhappy with their success?

(For the record, the answers are: not always, it should, maybe, depends on the success, I hope so, it can, it sure helps, I have no idea, and I don't even understand that last question.)

With so many people searching for success, happiness, and love, the question everyone wants answered is: *How do I get mine?*

Drugs and alcohol can make you happy. So can sex. And if you're having cocaine-fueled sex on a regular basis, I'd say you're pretty successful and I'm sure you'd say you're pretty happy. But there's a problem with using drugs for success and happiness: they're fucking expensive. And before you can say "cuckoo for Cocoa Puffs," you're broke. Worried you'll lose all the sensational benefits from the drugs you can no longer afford, you get a *second* job. But then you're so exhausted from working two jobs you need more yeyo just to keep going. Before you know it all the second job chedda is goin' to the dudeman pitchin' the mandanga. Now you're broke, miserable, *and* jonezing. Your white line fever requires a steady supply of snow— even if it means a life of crime to pay for the sleigh ride. So, you get a *third* job. However, while you *are* making money, you definitely aren't happy pulling gas station stick-up jobs at three in the morning. It's not your idea of a successful career not to mention the hours suck. And so you're right back to being unsuccessful and unhappy—with the capacity to only love dope.

As for sex? Well, many people spend their entire lives pursuing the physical act of love, expending all their energy, resources, and dignity on getting laid. And every time it happens, they consider themselves successful, happy, and possibly in love. But the carnal relations panacea also has its drawbacks.

If single, you're faced with the seemingly insurmountable task of seeming mountable. This includes the big three challenges of dating: keeping in physical shape, remaining employed, and consent. Perhaps you're in a committed relationship and think makin' bacon is a slam dunk every time. Well, you'd thunk wrong. The ass is always leaner on the other side. Raw doggin' excepted, coupling presents its own travails and tribulations. Top three among them: feigning interest whenever your significant other is talking, constant cajoling, and feigning interest whenever your significant other is talking.

But the most consequential impediment to sex as a viable option for success, happiness, and yes, even love, is *risk versus reward*. On balance, the capital expenditure required for the successful acquisition of kertang does sustain the low rate of return. With the massive amounts of time, resources, and effort required to cross the Tappin' Zee Ass Bridge, by the time you arrive, you'll be too exhausted to think about it let alone do it. The only surefire way for quick and easy procurement is to pay for it. But that means a lot more cash so you're right back to knocking off gas stations.

Other folks define success through their career, whether working for a company or themselves. Some people are even "workaholics"* finding success and happiness through their careers, working hard for long hours, often to the exclusion of everything

---

* Workaholism? Seriously? What kind of a person becomes addicted to *working*? Personally, if I'm going to be a "holic" it ain't gonna be from working too much. I'm choosing something more fun, like liquor or drugs or sex. Hell, even food or shopping makes more sense than working. I can think of so many worthier *aholics* to squander your life on: sleepaholic, TVaholic, pornoholic. But working too much...? Get the fuck outta my face.

and everyone in their life. But work as a conduit to a successful, happy life is rife with danger as well.

If you have your own business you worry about the volatility of the economy, duplicitous partners, slacker employees, and cutthroat competitors—any of which, through no fault of your own, can easily cause the demise of your enterprise. Conversely, being a cog in someone else's machine is no less perilous. Impracticable and insufferable demands are constantly made of you by your employer. Things like showing up on time, applying yourself, and doing what you're told. Working for the proverbial "man" or "woman" you're likely to be dispassionate about your endeavors as they serve to fulfill *someone else's* goals and dreams. Thus, remuneration becomes your paramount motivation, the aggregate of which usually leaves much to be desired. Other perils include asshole clients, asshole fellow employees, and the capricious nature of your boss (who is likely to be an asshole).

And if all that wasn't bad enough, one day, out of the blue, despite your loyal service, outstanding performance record, and not stealing shit when you clearly had the opportunity to do so, you can be laid off through no fault of your own or fired because of your drinking problem, drug addiction, or inter-office affair.

Religion/spirituality/faith are also pathways to success and happiness for many people who turn to ecclesiastical tomes purporting to be the single source of truth for success, happiness, and love in life. But there's one small catch: you have to die first. Meanwhile, until judgment day arrives, these religious organizations monitor everything you do, sitting in judgment and passing condemnation over the very fruits born of that success, happiness, and love: money, sex, drugs, pride, greed, wrath, envy, lust, gluttony, sloth. In short, everything that makes it worth being a human being.

Religion also demands effort. A LOT of it. In biblical proportions. It's a huge commitment that affects family, friends, and, most importantly, your leisure time—not to mention a complete overhaul of your entire lifestyle. Recreational alcohol consumption and sexual activity are heavily regulated, even frowned upon, and illicit drug use is all but forbidden.

There's also the financial commitment that comes with religion. You gotta cough green, usually on a weekly basis, to the tune of *ten percent of your gross income*! They call it a *tithe** but it's really just a fancy word for "God tax." *The Lord gave, and the Lord doth take that shit away* (Job 1:21). And believe you me, there's NO way around this one because instead of coming from convoluted government laws like the tax code, it comes from convoluted religious texts like the Bible.

> A tithe of everything from the land, whether grain
>   from the soil or fruit from the trees, belongs to
>   the Lord; it is holy to the Lord.
> *Leviticus 27:30*

How can you find a loophole in *that* tax law? You can't. Not when your shit *already* belongs to God. You can cheat on your taxes, but there's no way you can cheat on Yahweh.

In addition, with religion, there's reading involved. A lot of reading. Ungodly voluminous amounts of time-consuming, exhaustive reading. Remember, the vast majority of religions were made up back in the olden days when they didn't have audiobooks or podcasts so they had to *write* everything down. And for whatever reason, these fellowships cling to the written word like Tarantino to 35mm film.

However, there's an even more hazardous pothole in the Road to Damascus: there is *no* room for error. The stakes are hella high, like nothing else in your life. Say you screw up at

---

* The ten percent (10%) requirement specifically comes from the Hebrew translation of tithe or "ten."

your job. The worst that happens is you're fired. Unfortunate? Yes. But not insurmountable—you find another job. You pull a boner with your significant other? No big—the blindingly inherent codependent nature of relationships allows for timorous amorous reconciliation. (And if not, you can always find someone else just as good on the internet.)

But you fuck up in one of these religions, the payback is *forever*. Eternal perdition in the abode of the damned. No re-dos, no take-backs, no make-goods. Just licking Satan's scaly scrotum in perpetuity while burning in a pit of hellfire.*

Finally, many people turn to other human beings for success, happiness, and love—significant others, family members, friends, employers, politicians, clergy, psychics, authors, and escorts. It's definitely a viable option. It's been proven effective and is probably the most popular item on the menu. But it does come with its own potential complications, mainly the mercurial nature of people—and *that* is definitely out of your control. Once you make someone else the be-all and end-all of your success, happiness, and love, you've set yourself up for an inevitable downfall. Any one of them could join a religious cult, become an alcoholic, or even get hooked on drugs.

And if your spouse is at the center of your *everything universe*, congratulations! You've just placed yourself in an extra high-risk category. With the national divorce rate hovering around fifty

---

* Hellfire is waaaay worse than just normal fire. For reference, wood burns at 1,880.6 °F, gasoline at 1,878.8 °F, animal fat fire 1,472–1,652 °F, kerosene 1,814 °F, and charcoal at a toasty 2,534 °F. But science has proven that hellfire beats them all. In joint studies conducted by fireologists and clergy, hellfire was so hot, its temperature could not be recorded in measurements of Fahrenheit, Celsius, kelvin, or even Planck. Hellfire is so damn hot, scientists had to develop a new scale to measure it: *HF* (stands for HellFire... Yeah, science isn't really known for catchy marketing abilities). The heat of hellfire is approximately 666^{666} HF. You may not know how hot that actually is in earthly terms, but believe me when I say, *it's hella hot.*

percent,[1] it's likely your spouse will lose interest in you (seventy-five percent of divorces), have an affair (sixty percent of divorces), or simply become fed up with your shit (fifty-eight percent of divorces).[2] Would you invest anything with only a fifty percent chance of success? You'd be better off with cryptocurrency.

So, how about you? How do you define *your* success, *your* happiness, and *your* love? Have you thought about it? Let's do a fun, revealing, and easy visualization lessercise.

WARNING! EFFORT ALERT!
The following section involves thinking and writing. A modicum of time and effort on the part of you, the reader, will be required.

To ensure maximum benefit with minimal effort, please remember to follow these three rules:

1. Use a *single* piece of paper for the lessercise—more pages = more work.
2. Do *not* use a computer for the lessercises—embrace the *Three Ps*: paper, pencil, pen.
3. Do *not* overthink the lessercises—overthinking is overrated.

Grab a piece of paper and a writing utensil Go ahead. I'll wait right here.

.

.

.

Welcome back! With your paper and writing utensil, get comfortable in your chair, bed, car—wherever it is you're reading this. Clear your mind of everything—let all the outside distractions in the room or on the road melt away... Close your eyes and—

—*Crap.*

I told them to close their eyes.

Shit.

How do I get their attention? With their eyes closed they can't read this.

Banging loudly on my keyboard won't work.

Goddamnit. My first book and I'm already off to a bad start.

I knew I should've done an audiobook. Then I could just tell them to open their eyes. But audiobooks are so expensive to produce. All that production time, renting equipment, hiring technicians. Not to mention paying a narrator. I mean, I can't read it. I may have a face for radio but I got a voice for writing. I'm certainly regretting that decision now.

This just proves you gotta be careful what you write. People are influenced by the written word and they act on it. It's probably why they say the pen is mightier than the sword.

Oh, that's interesting: the word "sword" is "word" with an "s." The pen is mightier than the s-word.

That doesn't make any sense.

They have to open their eyes eventually. I'll just have to wait.

NOTE TO READER FOR WHEN YOU OPEN YOUR EYES...
If I'm not here I'm in the restroom, getting a drink, or checking my email. I'll be back in a few minutes. If you see this note BEFORE I return, PLEASE DO NOT CLOSE YOUR EYES AGAIN! With your eyes closed you can't read this book.
—MKJ

THANK GOD. You're reading this so it means you opened your eyes. Unfortunately, we're now behind schedule and have to make up the time.

Let's scratch the closing your eyes part—you get the point.

Just take a few moments and imagine what *success* looks like to you. Visualize what makes you successful.

Loads of money?

Your ream job? *(Whoops, that was a typo. It was supposed to be* dream *job. Actually, come to think of it, maybe you do want a* ream job *to be successful... I can go along with that.)*

Your ream home?

Is there a specific place in the world you live?

Are there things that *show* you're successful?

A fancy car?

A villa in Italy, or France, or Barbados, or all three?

Fabulous jewelry?

Expensive clothes?

A lickspittle mindlessly doing your bidding?

What are you *doing* as the "successful" you?

Running your own business?

Dating supermodels?

Wearing a top hat and monocle?

Perhaps your success is more immaterial...

Hard work?

Passion?

Journaling?

Goal setting?

Getting up early?

Think of everything that would make you "successful," write it down, then meet me back here.

.

.

.

Welcome back. You should now have a list of everything that defines the *successful you*.

Next is *happiness*.

What makes you happy?

Family?

Romantic partner?

Friends?

Pets?

What *things* make you happy?

Money? (It makes some folks successful *and* happy.)

Clothes?

Shoes?

Gadgets?

A ream job?

Where are you happiest?

The beach?

On vacation?

What are things you *do* that make you happy?

Working?

Playing?

Singing?

Dancing?

Having sex?

A creative pursuit?

Sleeping?

Laughing?

Hobbies?

Eating at restaurants?

Camping?

Going to the movies?

Watching TV?

Reading a book?

Writing a book?

Listening to music?

Recalling memories?

Seeking revenge on your enemies?

Are you happiest doing these things alone or with someone special?

If so, who?

Write down everything that makes you happy. When you finish, I'll still be right here, waiting for you...

.

.

.

Excellent! (Are you feeling a bit happier having visualized it?)

Care to take a shot at what's next? That's right, *love*. Picture whatever type of love you want in your life:

Emotional.

Sexual.

Free.

Platonic.

Personal.

Natural.

Transactional.

Voyeuristic.

Universal.

Cosmic.

There are so many flavors that you might even desire more than one. This is what we call a "love junkie." But hey, that's your business, Paisan. *

(However, for now, you might want to reign in the whole love thing by narrowing it down to one or two. Relationships are expensive and a lot of work (especially when they aren't working out) so I recommend not overdoing it and keeping it simple.)

Are you *in* love?

Being loved?

Or *doing* the loving?

Are you loving a specific person?

---

* Being that my mother was 50% Italian, that makes me Italian. So, I can use the term "Paisan" free of guilt, bigotry, prejudice, and cultural appropriation. In fact, because I am Italian, I can even tell offensive jokes that demean Italians and mock their rich culture and illustrious heritage by perpetuating the negative stereotypes that have burdened Italian Americans for nearly 150 years in the United States of America. I'm proud to be an Italian American.

Or is a specific person loving you?

Is it a specific thing from a specific person in a specific place?

Is it forever?

For now?

Or for the night?

Is some*thing* you love?

Money? (Not only does it make some folks feel successful and happy, some folks literally *love* it.)

Status?

A ream job?

Every detail that fully defines love in your life—write them all down.

While you're working on that, I'm gonna go make myself a drink, so if you're back before me, hang on, I'll be rejoining you shortly.

.

.

.

Look at that: both back at the same time. You have your love and I have my cocktail. In fact, I forgot to put that in my prompts —I LOVE my cocktails.

You now have the recipe for your success, happiness, and love. And there's no doubt it's right because *you* wrote it and you surely know better than anyone what makes you successful, happy, and in love.

So here's the last part of the lessercise: Pick up that piece of paper with your definitions on it ... Tear it up into tiny pieces... and toss them right into the garbage.

CHAPTER 3
THIS IS NOT THE LIFE I WANTED

People say nothing is impossible, but I do nothing every day.
—Winnie the Pooh

God, I wish I would've come up with that quote.
—M.K. Jackson

The self-help industrial complex promises positive, life-changing results through books, videos, podcasts, seminars, webinars, websites, social media, retreats, and live events. If it sounds too good to be true that's because it is. Read the fine print. Within it, you'll discover such underhanded undertakings as reading, goal setting, reading, journaling, more reading, and getting up in the morning hours earlier than you really need to just to read, set goals, and journal.

All this folderol is feasible if you're a preternaturally motivated adrenaline junkie insomniac. But what about real people? Folks like *us* with full-time jobs, social media addictions, and an imposing streaming video backlog? Most importantly, what about those of us who are simply *tired of trying so hard*? Why should we have to read and journal and set goals and get up early just to be successful? Forget about success, what about just being *happy*? If all people are indeed endowed with the certain unalienable right of happiness then why do we have to work so hard for it? I mean, it's a *right*, right?

There was a time in my (younger) life when I would "give it 110 percent" to "take it to the next level" in a "balls-to-the-walls" pursuit of personal potential, professional achievement, and spiritual fulfillment. I'd passionately squeeze every last drop of possibility, excellence, and adventure out of my life by getting up extra early to set goals, attach deadlines, and journal.

Allow me to paint you a picture. Each January 1st I took advantage of the fact that the first day of *my* new year was also the first day of the *world's* new year. With great ceremony, I'd purchase a new Moleskine classic hard cover 5" x 8.25" 12-Month Daily Planner. I'd spend the majority of my birthday journaling about the past year, reliving every triumph, challenge, and lesson for growth, applying it all to inform my journaling for the coming year's triumphs, challenges, and lessons for growth.

Once that was completed, I began the arduous task of grinding out new goals for the upcoming week, month, year, five years, ten years, twenty years, and fifty years. On my fiftieth birthday, I actually set fifty-year goals—like there was ever a chance I'd live to hit the century mark. And even if I do, I suspect my only goal will be to take a piss without it hurting— not conduct a thorough SWOT analysis on my business income. But that's how deep my sickness was.

I'd then transfer all my goals from my journal into quarterly spreadsheets and build data input formulas to track weekly progress, the results of which I'd break out onto color-coded, cross-referenced tabbed index cards to tape to my bathroom mirror, my refrigerator, my computer display, and my car dashboard.

Oh, but wait, I was just getting started.

With a clear vision of my next fifty years, I'd then break it out into a set of three journals, each focusing solely on a specific facet of my *awesome superlife*: personal development, professional benchmarks, and spiritual growth. For even greater specificity, each decade was given its own triptych detailing the mechanics of every goal's benefit, its pathway to completion, and due date. I was juggling *eighteen different journals* simultaneously, all of them accounting for every facet of my hopes, dreams, aspirations, and goals for the next half-century of my life.

I expended a monumental amount of time, effort, and resources to create a life of success, happiness, and love. It was my passion. My work. My raison d'être.

Yeah. Not anymore.

While prepping this book I looked back on all two hundred of those journals, cataloging and chronicling a fifty-year reach from who I was to who I wanted to be and you know what? I pretty much had the same goddamn goals every goddamn year: *Lose twenty pounds, make a million dollars, land my dream/ream job, own my dream home, meet my soul mate*—all of which I assumed would make me successful, happy, and loved.

Yeah. Not anymore.

I'm just too tired for all that crap. It's not that I gave up. It's just that I don't try so hard anymore. Now I say "EF-it" because I suffer from *Excellence Fatigue*. It's what happens when you're working so damned hard to be successful, happy, and loving that the only thing you're successful, happy, and loving at is working hard to be successful, happy, and loving. It was my personal battle with this *EFing* disease that led me to ponder these questions:

- *WHY aren't I more successful?*
- *WHY aren't I living "the dream?"*
- *WHY aren't I more fit and healthy?*
- *WHY don't I have a romantic relationship?*
- *WHY don't I earn more?*
- *WHY the hell aren't I happy?*

Is it simply because I don't work hard enough? Or get up early enough? Or make enough goals? Or set stricter deadlines? Or affirmate enough? Or meditate enough? Or journal enough? Or... could it possibly be something else..?

My Personal Story

I was a late bloomer. In everything. I even arrived late into this world. I was supposed to be a Christmas '63 baby but was born on New Year's Day, 1964.* Because my birthday was past the registration deadline, I began school late (I was always the oldest, yet somehow not the wisest, in my class). I didn't move out of my parents' house until I was twenty-two (practically middle-aged for leaving the nest back in those days). I started and graduated college late (in at twenty-one, out at twenty-six). I didn't get a "real" job until I was in my late thirties (and even then "real" is a fluid definition). I didn't start drinking [alcohol] until I was in my forties (but made up for lost time by skipping beer and wine and going straight to the hard stuff). I didn't get married for the first time until I was fifty. I didn't buy my first home until I was fifty-four. I didn't get my MFA until I was fifty-five. I didn't try marijuana until I was fifty-six. And for the sake of your psychological well-being and digestion, I won't even address when I finally lost my virginity (just know I'm nothing if not consistent).

Given all that, it follows that virtually every other aspect of my "adult life" got a late start as well. When I entered my forties I realized I was still living like someone twenty years my junior —someone like, say, *myself* when I was in *my* twenties...

---

* To the day he died, my dad insisted I still owed him 1963's income tax dependent exemption, something like $200 before he began compounding the interest for the following thirty years.

- I was still renting an apartment (rather than purchasing a home);
- all my jobs were freelance (like a heroin addict always looking for the next fix);
- I had low cash reserves in the bank (no emergency fund);
- I owed back taxes (from my freelancing 1099 gigs);
- I was a serial monogamist (one relationship after another but never married);
- I had no medical insurance (to treat my genetic gifts of high cholesterol and hypertension).

In a can't-take-your-eyes-off-the-car-wreck way, you may be wondering *what the hell's wrong with this guy*. Fortunately, we don't have enough pages, time, or excuses to go into that here. But suffice it to say that the ill-advised pursuit of occupation in the creative arts long overstayed its welcome, providing me with a decades-long alibi from maturity and responsibility. I likely would have continued to drift aimlessly for God knows how much longer had it not been for the intervention of fate: I met someone.

The profound effect of a romantic relationship on one's life cannot be underestimated. At its best, an affair of the heart acts like a windshield defroster, blowing away the foggy foresight and giving you a clear view of life's road ahead. At its worst? Well, we'll get to that a little later.

After a mere eight years of courtship, I gradually began to consider the possibility that she *might*, just *might*, be "the one." Not wanting to jump the gun, I waited two more years just to be sure. After which, a loud *bang!* went off in my head and I thought *maybe we should get married*. That impulsive ten-year decision reverberated throughout every aspect of my arrested adolescence, sounding the alarm that it was time to grow up and be an "adult." The best way I knew to accomplish such a seismic shift in my life was to attain all the trappings of a successful, happy, and loving adult life which I had long been dodging. So I did what anyone hellbent on taking their life to the next level does: I journaled. Page after page after page. I mean, I journaled the shit out of my life. Journaling where I'd been, journaling where I was, and, journaling where I needed to go: Adultland—population: *me.*

I had read, watched, and listened to enough personal improvement books, courses, podcasts, and seminars to know that my first step was *goal setting.* Goals, as I learned, are the cornerstone of self-improvement because they are tangible; they create manageable steps, maintain focus, motivate, measure progress, promote accountability, give a feeling of accomplishment, blah blah blah, quack quack quack. *Hot diggity was I sold on goals!*

As I began my goal-setting workshop for the successful/happy/loving adult me, I decided to keep it simple, which meant current goals only; no five-year goals, ten-year goals, or twenty-year goals. My father and both my grandfathers all died between the ages of forty-six and fifty-four, so the way I saw it at age fifty I was already living on borrowed time. At any second the Devil could call in his chit, cash me out, and take me home.

As far as the goals, knowing which ones to set was actually pretty easy; I simply listed all the adult-life things I *didn't* have that I *should* have. Thankfully, all my friends were already married and living like adults so I had role models for inspiration. I amazed myself at how quickly I set my goals. They just poured out of me. In no time I set **six goals** necessary to become a successful, happy, and loving adult:

My Successful, Happy, and Loving Adult Life Goals Checklist

1. A well-paying, permanent-position job with benefits (a "real" job).
2. A committed, long-term relationship (marriage).

3. Purchase a house with a yard and a garage (just like the one I grew up in) to build equity and not flush rent $ down the toilet.
4. Bank at least one year of living expenses (financial security).
5. Medical insurance (physical health).
6. Spiritual harmony (emotional, psychological, and spiritual health).

I was pretty proud of those goals (regardless of the fact that it took me five decades to figure them out). They were simple, clear, and realistic. No more of that pie-in-the-sky folly that got me into this mess to begin with. *These* goals were a realistic balance between human aspirations and creature comforts—the ideal blueprint to make me a successful, happy, loving adult. With the ink on my journal pages barely dry, I fervently attacked my goals. Within two years, I had achieved the following:

1. A well-paying, full-time, management-position job with benefits (including sick days and vacation time). *Check!*
2. As a result of achieving #1, I was less stressed and more rested, no longer having to look for new work every day. *Check!*
3. I got engaged and then married. *Check!*
4. I settled my tax debt. *Check!*
5. I tended to my health—dental, vision, and medical. *Check!*
6. With two incomes, we were saving more money than I ever had accumulated alone. *Check!*
7. My wife and I were looking to purchase a home (and stop paying rent). *Half check!*
8. All this put me in personal and spiritual harmony within myself. *Check!*

By the end of that two-year period, I was successful, happy, and in love. I proved one can achieve all one's goals—as long as one puts one's mind to it, works hard, and journals like a fool. Having crushed it on the short-term goals, I was now ready to design the five-, ten-, and twenty-year goals. I was on a goal roll and nothing could stop me.

Then came the dick punch that was 2016. I never knew what hit me.

In June of that year, the first bomb dropped. Shy of our second anniversary, the marriage was over. While I did not want the divorce, I knew I was equally culpable. Nevertheless, I was devastated. Coming from a divorced family, I *really* wanted to succeed in my marriage, but it was not to be. The legal part went smoothly, but the emotional part was a bitch. Talk about a failure. As I saw it, this one put me in the Hall of Fame.

Along with the marriage, so too went my hopes of buying a house. Without dual incomes, I was priced out of the Los Angeles single-family home real estate market. I moved out of our apartment and got my own place, a quintessential L.A. bungalow (shit, back to renting). To alleviate some of the loneliness brought on by my newly single life, I adopted a roommate: an adult female cat named Posie (whom I quickly taught to shake hands on command). Even with all this change and continuing to endure the divorce process, I somehow managed to keep on top of my job—probably because I didn't want to lose another part of my newly assembled adult life.

After a few months, things began to settle into a "new normal-ish" for me—although it was a little sadder and a little less hopeful than my previous normal. But hey, at least I was still alive! Then again, this was only July. 2016 still had five more months left to go.

Earlier in the year, I began having vision problems—spots of brightness and focusing difficulties. My ophthalmologist ran several tests and found nothing of concern. He gave me some eyedrops and told me to check back in a couple of weeks if my eyesight didn't improve. It didn't. He brought me in for more tests. Negative. Negative. Negative. And negative. Having exhausted all the tricks in his testy sack, he made his final prognosis.

"It's probably something you're just going to have to live with. I'll give you some eye drops which should alleviate it some."

And with that, Doctor A-game was on to the next patient. But as I left the examination room, the ophthalmic technician turned to me and quietly said:

"You know... You might want to have a neurologist take a look at you."

I wasn't sure a tech would know more than an ophthalmologist but having exhausted the ocular options I thanked him for his suggestion and told him I would—even though I still figured my vision problems were caused by the stress of the divorce, not brain strain.

Apparently, I'm a lousy doctor because it wasn't stress.

By late September, after meeting with several neurologists and undergoing a battery of neurological tests including a CT scan, and another MRI (this one with and without contrast), I was given an appointment at the hospital. Whenever you're *given* an appointment you didn't request, man, you just know it's gonna be some serious shit.

The nurse escorted me into an examination room where I took a seat and waited for what seemed like another hour. Finally, the door opened and Dr. Daniels, the neurosurgeon in charge of my care entered. He was followed in by another doctor... then another... and another... and still another. The five-member neurology team faced me wearing their white coats and straight faces. I knew this wasn't going to be good. It never is when there are *five* doctors. It's difficult enough getting to see *one* doctor, but *five* of them to see you of their own volition? Man, you just know it's gonna be some serious shit. Dr. Daniels calmly looked me in the eye and gave it to me straight:

"You have a brain tumor."

My gut dropped into my crotch, like that first big dive on a roller coaster. I just sat there in shock, speechless. What do you say to a doctor who tells you you have a brain tumor? Well, I can tell you what I said.

"How big is it?

Yep. Out of all the questions I could've asked, like "Am I going to go blind?" "Is it cancerous?" "Can you remove it?" "How long do I have to live?" Or even "Does my insurance cover it?" I wanted to know the tumor's size because, of course, with my vast neurological knowledge, knowing its size would help me formulate my own prognosis, treatment, and recovery plan.

"Two point three centimeters," Dr. Daniels told me.

"Over two centimeters?" I offered. "Jesus."

Truth was, I had no idea how big the tumor was because I had no fucking idea how big a centimeter was—and I still don't. I'm an American. We don't know fuck-all about the metric system. They tried to foist that bullshit on us back in the early 70s, and we threw it right back in their fat faces. ADVICE TO DOCTORS: When you tell a patient like me—a product of the United States of America school system—how big the bad shit is in our body that you have to remove, don't use the goddamn metric system. Aim a little lower and use the Imperial System of Measurement. Better yet, compare it to an object the size of which we are familiar, like *Mr. Jackson, your brain tumor is the size of a red seedless grape.* Or *When was the last time you ate a "Cuttie" clementine? I ask because, for you, that's like eating your brain tumor.* See? MUCH simpler and understandable.

So we're now like, ten minutes into this consultation, and I still have no idea whether I'm going to die, go blind, or both. Pointing to the MRI, Dr. Daniels showed me how the tumor was pressing against my optic nerve (causing the vision disturbance). Simply stated, it had to be removed, or I would go blind (okay, at least I got *that* question answered). But Dr. Daniels did have some good news: there was little-to-no chance the tumor was cancerous. If I had to have a brain tumor, I got the right one (seriously, you do need to celebrate even the little wins).

Looking back on that day, I'm still surprised at how calm I remained. I suppose I should have been in shock or scared shitless, but I was so preoccupied with the divorce and the size of a centimeter I wasn't all that worried about the tumor. Then again, maybe I was so alarmed by the tumor I wasn't all that concerned with the divorce. It was like mutually assured indifference. I wound up just being numb to everything.

A quick two weeks later in early October, I was in the hospital, entrusting the contents of my noggin to Dr. Daniels and his amazing team. They wheeled me into the operating room. The gas-passer filled me with anesthesia. I slowly dozed off and immediately awakened. That was it—it was over in an instant. During that instant, in fact, six hours had passed. When I came to, the nurse at my side told me the surgery was successful. I felt completely normal except for one thing: I was craving McDonald's hamburgers—even odder given the fact I hadn't eaten meat, McDonald's or otherwise, in nearly twenty-five years. I immediately suspected that McDonald's was somehow involved in the manufacturing of that anesthesia. It sure would explain Happy Meals.

During my post-op visit, Dr. Daniels informed me that unfortunately, due to the location of the tumor, they weren't able to remove all of it (something to do with the carotid artery and not wanting to cut into brain tissue). As a result, the tumor's (re)growth would have to be continually monitored and that meant at least two MRIs annually. Depending on the speed at which the remaining tumor grew, there was at least a fifty/fifty chance I would likely require another surgery in three to five years.

Now, I've always been a firm believer in the old adage that *if there's anything more unappealing than one brain surgery, it's two brain surgeries.* So while grateful for the success of this operation, the thought of tempting fate with another one was rather depressing. The good news was my recovery went well (sans one false alarm regarding leaking brain fluid) and within six weeks my life was back to *new normal*.

Come December 31, I was happy to kick 2016 in the ass on its way out the door. It had easily been the worst year of my life. So bad, in fact, on my 2016 income tax returns, I wrote my entire life off as a loss. But that somehow triggered an audit, resulting in me owing the IRS *three* years of back living. Go figure.

2017 continued to test me physically, psychologically, and emotionally while also chipping away at the "adult life" I had built. The highlight reel:

- My financial savings dwindled—mostly from medical bills.
- My mother fell in her bathroom and was hospitalized.
- I had an MRI every six months—the tumor was growing back at an above-average rate.
- My mom's physical condition declined for months as dementia took hold of her.
- My divorce was finalized—the day after Christmas 2017. Happy Holidays!

Eager to initiate a positive event in my life, I decided to try to buy my own home. Although my financials were good, the purchasing power of my salary alone precluded a house. So, I lowered my sights and split the difference. Nine months and thirteen offers later, I bought a townhouse in Los Angeles. I was happy and grateful to finally be a homeowner but man, I really wanted a house with a yard and a garage just like the one I grew up in (I know, quality problems).

Shortly after moving into my new place, my cat, Posie began losing weight and withdrawing from me. I chalked it up to the stress and anxiety of the new digs.

Apparently, I'm as lousy a veterinarian as I am a doctor because it wasn't stress.

Posie had developed a tumor on her kidney. The veterinarian explained that the size of the tumor (again, in goddamned centimeters) precluded any treatment, including surgery, and recommended euthanizing Posie ASAP. Knowing something about tumors myself, I sought a second opinion. Sadly, it too returned a negative prognosis. To save Posie from further suffering I was forced to put her to sleep days later. Not only was losing Posie crushing, it let loose the Kraken of suppressed emotions from my divorce, my brain tumor, and being alone in a townhouse that was supposed to be my marital dream home. I bawled like a baby.

Meanwhile, my mother's health began to rapidly decline. Physically she was bedridden, mentally she had dementia, and emotionally I was a wreck. For the next few months, I gladly used my vacation time traveling to the San Francisco Bay Area to visit her in the skilled nursing facility, tending to her as best I could, which really meant just being her son. This was the woman who raised me, fed me, nursed me when I was sick, introduced me to The Beatles (with her *Revolver* album—yeah, mom was pretty hip), and took me to my first concert in 1979 (the Bee Gees). Yet, in some ways, she was no longer my mom. Her personality had faded away. While she remembered me, she had no idea where she was or how she got there—but she had perfect recollection of the distant past. I'd sit bedside with her and we'd reminisce about things decades prior like it was yesterday. Every so often she'd drift away from me into her own world. It was heartbreaking watching her "pick" the flowers off her printed bed sheet and place them on an imaginary shelf beside her bed.

As 2019 drew to a close, I was stuck with the worst blow yet. My mom passed away. She was only seventy-two.

I had always just assumed she would get better. My mom was a fighter. She had recovered from *TWO* goddamned brain surgeries—either of which was much worse than mine. One for an aneurism, the other for a golf ball-sized tumor in the middle of her cerebral hemispheres. So yeah, I assumed she'd recover from this too.

The hospital called me that morning to tell me she was now just hours away from passing. I didn't even finish the call and I certainly didn't take time to pack anything. I hauled ass to the airport, flew from Los Angeles to the San Francisco Bay Area, rented a car, and was violating several traffic laws racing to get to her when, just five minutes away, the nurse called to tell me my mom had died. Goddamned, son of a bitch timing.

Four minutes later, I ran into her room as if by getting to her faster I'd somehow get a final minute or two with her still alive. She was in her bed, covered with a sheet when I saw her. I stared at the contours of her body in the sheet, running the last few hours through my mind, noting every moment when I could've gotten those *four* minutes back, IF. IF that nurse had just called me *two* minutes earlier. IF I were three rows closer to the door I would've been off the plane *one* minute earlier. IF I had beat that very happy couple to the rental car counter I could've saved *three* minutes right there. It took them forever to rent their damn car. No one's in a hurry when they're happy. Goddamned, fucking timing.

There wasn't much business to tend to; my mom didn't have very much. While she told me she wanted to be cremated, she never said what to do with her remains. This wasn't a problem though because I had the perfect place.

My mom was a big fan of classic Hollywood movies. Years earlier when she visited me in Los Angeles, I mapped out an "Old Hollywood" tour for her, taking her to sights she'd seen in movies or read about in the many Hollywood books I gave her. Of all the places we visited, Paramount Pictures was her favorite —she loved seeing those gates she'd seen so often in movies. For years after her visit, she was still talking about it. So I made the decision to inter her in Los Angeles at the Hollywood Forever

Cemetery. Her outdoor niche is located directly behind the Paramount Pictures lot, high enough that if she turns her head ninety degrees to the right she can see those very Paramount gates she loved so much.

2020 began with my latest MRI indicating my tumor had grown back to the size requiring removal. Once again, I found myself preparing for brain surgery. But this time, I felt like an old pro. I learned a lot from my first surgery that would make this second one so much more enjoyable. For instance, did you know you can ask for extra cups of apple sauce with your meals? I didn't (not the first surgery anyway)—a wrong I vowed to right during my second go 'round. And you can also ask for coffee at *any* time, not just at mealtime. So, I called the hospital the day before I was admitted and told them to start brewing, 'cause Jackson and his tumor are coming to town—and *the joe is gonna flow.*

Dr. Daniels was back for an encore and scheduled his performance for late April. I prepared for my absence at work and equipped my home for my recovery period.

Then, just weeks before my operation, the COVID-19 pandemic hit. As the shutdowns began, my surgery was canceled until... whenever. But it wasn't my operation I was concerned about. I was employed at a travel industry magazine. The lion's share of our advertising revenue was from cruise lines, hotels and resorts, and airlines. And you know what happened to them when the 'Rona rolled in. I watched in dread as ad revenue quickly dried up. My company immediately instigated pay cuts, furloughs, and layoffs. I knew I wasn't going to escape this unharmed when I received an email from the company's vice president requesting a phone call with me first thing the next morning at 8:00. This guy hadn't said two words to me in nearly a decade, so I figured we weren't going to discuss who's bringing what to the holiday party. Within twenty-six seconds of our call, I was laid off—permanently. I even remember the date: April 1, 2020—April Fool's Day. The same day my mortgage was due. The net gain of being a homeowner became a net burden with its mortgage, property taxes, and insurance premium. Also gone along with my job was my medical insurance, just in time for that second surgery—which I guess didn't matter since the pandemic closed the hospitals. But I still needed my cholesterol and blood pressure meds.

It took me two years to build my successful, happy, loving life—and not much longer than that to lose it. I was unemployed, divorced, my mom died, my cat died, and I was sheltering in place during the worst pandemic in a hundred years with a mortgage I could no longer afford. At least I had my health (well, aside from high cholesterol, hypertension, and that brain tumor). Man, I really wasn't looking forward to starting all over at age fifty-six.

I realize that the depression dump I just laid on you may seem like an off-the-rails pity party, filled with quality problems and ill-proportioned responses. Many people (including those of you reading this) must endure such crises in life—and many of them far more devastating than those I faced. But the truth is, there was a buffed-up, shiny silver lining in all of this for me: I was forced to reexamine the unexamined life I hadn't been examining.

Once I got past the shock of the events and the fear they caused, I came to realize that what happened was out of my control. I ultimately held no sway over whether another person wished to remain married to me or not. It was a pandemic that took my job, not my performance. My brain tumor was unavoidable. My mom's passing was not something I could have prevented. And little Posie's tumor was unavoidable. That didn't mean all those things would have zero emotional toll on me. It only meant I had permission to release myself from the responsibility of their loss. But I wasn't quite there just yet.

Given this way of looking at things, I couldn't technically classify myself as a "failure" yet I was not successful, happy, or with love in my life. That paradox was continually gnawing away at me: if the goals that made me successful, happy, and in love were truly out of my control then I was either doomed to be a victim of failure or a fortuitous recipient of indiscriminate success—either way it seemed I was impotent in forging my destiny.

Regardless of how I would right my ship, I had a transcendent realization: it would not involve any more goddamn goals. The way I saw it, goals were the cause of this entire mess. When everything I achieved from those goals was gone, so too was my success, happiness, and love. Further analysis of my so-called goals provided these five important observations:

1. Baked into the attainment of some of my goals was the *necessary consent* of at least one other person over whom I had *no* control.

2. Required for the achievement of some of my goals was the *cooperation of things and/or events* over which I had no control.

3. Ironically, the same goals, that when attained, made me successful, happy, and in love, now revoked made me feel like a failure.

4. I questioned whether I even set the right goals to begin with—ultimately determining they may have been inherently flawed at conception.

5. Having put so much time and effort into pursuing and achieving my goals, I was now so exhausted and dejected that I didn't have the tenacity to start all over again now that it was all gone.

While pondering these conclusions, I was reminded of the old adage: *You cannot direct the wind, but you can control your sails.* The goals were the sails, and I didn't control them when I should have—*while I was setting them.* They came from those six *why* questions I shared with you at the beginning of this chapter. So what went wrong? Well, it wasn't the answers, it was the questions. *You can't get the right answers if you're asking the wrong questions.*† Instead of asking *why*, better to ask *what*:

- *What* does it mean for me to succeed?
- *What* are my dreams?
- *What* would make me fit and healthy?
- *What* makes the perfect relationship for me?
- *What* is the amount I want to earn?
- *What* the hell will make me truly happy?

The simple rephrasing of the questions shifted the definitions from passive acceptance to proactive possibility in a way that not only empowered me to control the sails but also the wind, the boat, and the ocean (metaphorically speaking).

While pondering these new questions I was struck with **Three Epiphanies**. It would be this triumvirate of revelations that would guide me on the path to reclaiming my success, happiness, and love while providing the foundation for this book.

---

* This quote, in one variation or another, has throughout the years been attributed to numerous persons including Cora L. V. Hatch, Thomas Sheridan, George Whyte-Melville, A. B. Kendig, Ella Wheeler Wilcox, Bertha Calloway, Jimmy Dean, Dolly Parton, and Thomas S. Monson, and now, me.

† Attributed to Mark Victor Hansen, this quote is a variant of the myriad "question/answer" chestnuts grown by the self-help industrial complex including, but hardly limited to: *Change a question, change your life* (Tony Robbins), *If you ask the wrong question, of course, you get the wrong answer* (Amory Lovins), *It doesn't matter what answers you get if you ask the wrong questions* (Jim Thompson), *An approximate answer to the right problem is worth a good deal more than an exact answer to an approximate problem* (John Tukey), and *If you get people asking the wrong questions, you don't have to worry about the answers* (Thomas Pynchon—but sometimes incorrectly attributed to Hunter S. Thompson).

CHAPTER 4

EPIPHANY ONE: I'M TRYING TOO HARD

You never fail until you stop trying.
—Albert Einstein

You stop trying and you'll never fail.
—M. K. Jackson

Throughout my life, I always tried *too* hard.
In *everything*.

I tried too hard to be happy. I tried too hard for professional success. I tried too hard in relationships—platonic and romantic (especially romantic). But most of all, I tried too hard to please people. As a consequence, my *effort-to-results ratio* was way out of whack. The time, work, and resources I invested in any given pursuit far outweighed the minuscule tangible results I achieved.

Just as frustrating were the instances in which the results were substantial but fleeting. In other words: which is worse, never earning a million dollars or earning a million dollars and then losing it?

Most of us try too hard. The amount of effort we put into life and its pursuits is often excessive to the point of being counterproductive. We blindly accept, without evidence or application, these baseless axioms:

trying more = success/happiness/love; trying less = misery/failure/loneliness.

I'm here to tell you there is no scientific proof I've developed to substantiate those claims. And that's the basis of my first epiphany.

Arousing Your IRE

Before I continue, I wish to stress that not trying so hard does *not* mean throwing in the towel or even half-assing it. It means sticking to it and putting forth *some* effort—just not to the point where you cross the line from *reasonable attempt* to *ineffectual endeavor*. To avoid such ruination, you must provoke your IRE— *Internal Regulator of Effort*, a seventh sense (the one after that one that lets you see dead people) essential to detecting the destructive state of being fueled by delusions of ability and achievement in which the misplaced, ill-proportioned expenditure of resources rules out any possibility of beneficial returns.

As with any other extrasensory ability you possess (like a "gut feeling" or "x-ray vision"), you naturally already have your IRE. The problem is that you've been trained to betray it (by whom and for what reasons will be discussed in chapter four: Make It a Rule to Value Your Beliefs). For now, to stop the *hemorrhaging of trying* in your life, you must raise your IRE.

What follows are **five precepts** to help you counteract wasteful expenditures of effort. Whenever you feel yourself sinking in the quicksand of infertile endeavor, ask yourself if any of these maxims apply to your pursuit at hand, and if so, you should continue. The more that do, the more you don't.

1. Truth is, you don't *really* want whatever it is you're putting so much time and effort into.

As you will discover in the subsequent chapters of this book, often what we choose to focus on and pursue comes from a source other than ourselves. We have been subconsciously programmed to *believe* it's something we need and/or want. It's like the Macarena. Because everyone in the world was doing the Macarena you thought you should, too. You didn't actually *want* to do the Macarena (no one did) but before you knew it, there you were: *Heeeeeey, Macarena!*

Say your parents always wanted you to be a doctor. Your entire childhood they hammered away at you to go to medical school. But you wanted to be a musician. Fearing you would be throwing your life away on "a silly hobby," your parents showed you several PowerPoint presentations of homeless, heroin-addicted failed musicians forced to turn tricks for their fix on skid row. Everyone told you your parents were right: it *is* better to be a doctor than a heroin-addicted failed musician turning tricks for a fix on skid row. Therefore, you acquiesced and gave up on music. (Credit where credit's due, those *really* were some very persuasive PowerPoints.) So you found yourself in medical school, trying harder than you ever tried in your entire life. But all the work, time, and resources you invested in your studies didn't cut the mustard because science, math, and, studying (AKA "academia") just ain't your strong suit. No shame. Some people are doctors, and some are heroin-addicted musicians turning tricks for their next fix on skid row.

As a result, you knowingly (or unknowingly) sabotaged yourself. Your fate-to-fail was sealed and you became a heroin-addicted failed medical student turning tricks for their fix on skid row—a lifestyle that would have been at least a bit more tolerable if you had music in your life.

None of this would have happened had your IRE been raised.

2. You are not qualified, prepared, or otherwise cut out for it.

Sometimes in life, we fail to achieve because we're just not good enough—and simply trying harder will not change that. It could be lack of education, smarts, physicality, or plain old ambition. This is very difficult for most of us to accept—especially if we've been told from childhood that we can be and do *anything* as long as we put our minds to it and work hard enough. Unfortunately, that's a wide-ass truckload load of hard-packed horseshit barreling down a narrow rural road headed straight for you.

Personally, I'm sure no matter how hard I try, I won't be the first fifty-eight-year-old centerfielder for the Los Angeles Dodgers. I've made peace with the fact that this book won't win me a Pulitzer. And I know I lack the disposition, intelligence, drive, and fortitude to be a brain surgeon. Sure, I'm fairly smart and I have *some* ambition, but *medical school*? *Ehhh...* I don't think so. When my IRE is up, it tells me that no matter how hard I try, my medical school career would just be another eight years of "needs to apply himselfs"—not exactly the academic legacy one looks for in a noggin doctor.

Hello, I'm Dr. Jackson, your neurosurgeon. I need to apply myself. Now let's get crackin' on that skull a yers.

It's more likely I'd become a heroin-addicted failed medical student turning tricks for his fix on skid row. None of this upsets me anymore because there are plenty of *ability-appropriate* things I am cut out for and can spend my time successfully pursuing.

3. You are not connected.

You applied for your dream job—great interview, impressive résumé, unimpeachable references, and not one restraining order that still appears on your record. But the reality is you never had a chance in your pants of getting that job. The company always planned on hiring from within—within the CEO's family—but they had to stage that dog-and-pony-show application process to meet the equal opportunity employment requirements.

Being outside the inner circle will block your pathway to success and happiness and trying harder will *not* get you in. You don't know the right person. You have the wrong alma mater. You weren't in the right fraternity or sorority. Or your friend who recommended you just didn't have the juice.

When the fix is in, your loss is predetermined. You may recoil at such a fatalistic assessment of the situation, but the truth is it's a *good* thing. Just think of how liberating it is knowing that no extra amount of trying could have ever tipped the scales in your favor. It releases you from the burden that you didn't try hard enough.

4. Luck.

That serendipity is instrumental in prosperity is quite an unpopular notion with the self-help industrial complex—and it's easy to see why. After rising extra-early every day to journal, set goals, recite affirmations, and just be totally awesome, the notion that dumb luck could somehow be a determining factor in achieving success, happiness, and yes, even love is offensively contradictory to self-actualization dogma. Yet when asked, the most successful, happy, and in-love people will often tell you that luck did indeed play a part [and a quite often large one] in their good fortune.

Forbes magazine featured a study from the University of Catania in Italy that explored the role luck plays in success and happiness. The researchers created a computer simulation model that assigned people a certain level of talent made up of skill, ability, and intelligence. Talent was allocated randomly throughout the population sample with a general bell-curve-style distribution.

The model tracked each person through a forty-year working life, with random lucky and unlucky events throughout. The study found that lucky events increased each individual's wealth whereas unlucky events reduced it. At the end of the simulation, each person was ranked according to wealth achieved, with the researchers able to examine each person's life to ascertain how that wealth came about and whether any successful characteristics emerged. While the wealth was broadly distributed, it was not distributed according to talent. The article notes:

The simulations the team ran were able to accurately reflect the wealth distribution we see in the real world, but what was really inter-

esting is it wasn't those regarded as the most talented that became the wealthiest, but rather those regarded as the luckiest.[1]

Well, what d'ya know? Kismet rears its ugly head to prove a lucky break can exceed even skill, ability, and intelligence. And all this time you thought trying extra hard would be the secret to your success and happiness when actually you should've been purchasing horseshoes, rabbit's feet, four-leaf clovers, wishbones, and fortune cookies.

5. The Law of Diminishing Trying.

Trying, like eating, drinking, deviant sexual behavior, and illicit drug use is all about moderation. While the trying you put into something might indeed net some nugatory results, there also comes a literal point when trying becomes inefficacious—even depreciatory. This is the basis of *The Law of Diminishing Trying*.

This principle asserts that if the trying (*variable* resource) in pursuit of an objective is increased while all other factors (*fixed* resources) remain constant, a point will be reached where supplemental trying will actually yield a zero-net gain. In fact, efforts beyond that zero point will eventually produce a *negative* effect that subtracts from progress previously gained.

An example of The Law of Diminishing Trying is what researchers refer to as *The Exorcism Allotment Modality*. It goes like this: one exorcist and his assistant (*variable* resources) are casting out a demon (*fixed* resource) from a *demoniac*, AKA the possessed person (*fixed* resource). Unfortunately, the exorcism is failing because a union exorcist can only work eight hours a day (*fixed* resource) before suffering *demonic fatigue* (it's a thing, Google it). But the devil can possess all day and night because he has no union (that's why he's the devil).

So this leaves fourteen to sixteen hours remaining each day where the possessed person is just sitting around being all possessed and evil with no exorcising taking place. To resolve this deficit in expulsion productivity, an additional exorcist and assistant (*variable* resources) are summoned. Although two more people are now on the payroll (including benefits), eight hours per day have been added to the exorcism workflow, contributing to a more efficient and expedient expulsion of the demon.

With this double-up exorcising being so productive, a *third* exorcist and assistant are mobilized to fill in the dormant four to six hours a day and provide breaks to the other two teams. (To refill holy water, wash vomit off their cassocks, hydrate, take power naps, etc.)

Now they're exorcising 'round the clock so that demon's going to be flushed out sooner, freeing up the aforementioned resources to tackle other exorcisms.

But let's take it a step further and add a *fourth* exorcist and assistant. Would that increase the expulsion productivity even more? According to the Law of Diminishing Trying, the answer is a Satan-sized *hell NO*. While the *variable* resources (exorcists and assistants) were increased, the *fixed* resources (demoniac, demon, exorcism, exorcists, twenty-four hours in a day) remain constant. Where and when would the fourth exorcist and assistant work? We already have six-orcists kicking demon ass twenty-four/seven.

The new exorcist and assistant would only be in the way, stepping on each other's prayer responses, spilling holy water on each other, and losing their place in the Rituale Romanum. We'd have exorcists literally tripping over one another. Additionally, with a redundant exorcist and assistant, there would be an exorteam sitting around doing nothing but wasting time, money, and fancy garments.

You can see from this true-life example that trying *more* does not necessarily mean trying *better* (especially when the unholy Dark Father is involved).

There Is No "I" in "Try"

No matter how creative, ingenious, or strategic my efforts, they are inevitably met with forces of resistance dispassionate to my causes and partisan to their own. Pre-epiphany one, when I ran into a wall I would attempt to *try* my way over, under, around, or through it. When those attempts failed, I would dig in under the delusional influence that I could bend the opposing forces to my will through sheer trying—but I never could. So, I'd blame myself; *I wasn't smart enough, I wasn't strong enough, I was possessed, I didn't know the right people*, and on and on and on. I could have saved myself a lot of time, tears, and trips to the liquor store had I only realized I was trying *too* hard. To para-coin a phrase, *try lesser, not harder*.

CHAPTER 5
EPIPHANY TWO: I'VE BEEN DRIVING SOMEONE ELSE'S CAR

If you don't design your own life plan, chances are you'll fall into someone else's plan. And guess what they have planned for you? Not much.

—Jim Rohn

That guy's right.

—M. K. Jackson

You know how it is when you drive someone else's car for the first time? You sit in the driver's seat and the car just feels like it's made for someone else (because it is).

The seat is too high, too low, too far back, or up too close. The steering wheel is either jammed into your lap or tilted up so high it blocks your view of the speedometer. You look into the rearview mirror and see the back seat or the ceiling. And the side mirrors offer a view of the sky or the ground. But worst of all is that malodorous pine tree car air "freshener" hanging on the rearview mirror. What's that smell—whorehouse bathroom on fire? The putrefying stench is in your eyes, nose, and mouth, making you sicker and sicker to your stomach with every breath you take.

You roll down the windows, fire up the engine, and drive off.

Changing lanes, you nearly clip a car because you didn't see it in the inexactly adjusted mirrors. The seat's so far back, you have trouble maintaining the correct speed because you can't reach the gas pedal—or the seat's jammed so far forward you can't move your foot to the brake fast enough and you almost take out a pedestrian.

Given this car is so difficult to operate you decide to bypass the dangers of city driving and hit the highway where it's open road as far as the eye can see. You set the cruise control since you can't effectively work the pedals. Now you're on autopilot. Mile follows mile. Your mind drifts. You lose track of time. An hour passes. Then another. The monotony of the road speeding under the car is hypnotizing. *You are getting sleeeepyyyy.* To stay awake, you turn on the radio. It's set to a station that plays music you *hate*. Who listens to this crap?! (The persona who owns the car, obviously). By now, the lumbar-pulverizing seat has torpedoed your back and you're in pain. You can't take any more of this goddamn music. But when you turn off the radio, you start to doze again. You fight sleep. Lose track of time. Before you know it, you've driven hundreds of miles in someone else's car. You're lost, tired, and in pain with no recollection how you got where you are and even less of an idea how to get back.

Getting Behind the Wheel

The day after I was laid off from my job of nine years, I woke up and everything hit me at once. No job. No wife. No cat. No mom. Mounting medical bills. And a brain tumor that kept popping up like a Whack-a-Mole. I was a complete failure in success, happiness, and love. This was *not* the life I wanted.

Truth be told, I wasn't feeling sorry for myself. I wasn't feeling *anything*. I was *numb*. At age fifty-six, I was given the distinct displeasure of having to start life all over. Shit. It was a bitch doing it the *first* time around, making the thought of having to do it again excruciating. I simply didn't have the motivation to do it. I didn't have the motivation to do *anything*. Well, anything except YouTube 1950s and 60s breakfast cereal TV commercials, re-binge-watch *Mad Men*, and devour bowls of Peanut Butter Cap'n Crunch. Before I knew it, a month slipped by. Then another. And another. The pounds packed on. Depression overcame me. And my world became smaller.

To quote 1980s poet/philosopher Robbie Nevil, *When you're down there's just one way to go. Now sing it!* (Actually, the answer is "up." C'est La Vie.) And I was surely down as far as I could go. So, I thought it would be advantageous to my sanity if I nicked a tool from the self-help industrial complex and compiled an inventory of everything I should be grateful for—AKA a *gratitude list*. I was determined to get *something* out of all that personal improvement bullshit I was choking on. I mean, it got me into this mess, it should get me out. I focused specifically on things I (still) had that could make me feel *successful* and *happy*. (I'd hold off on the love part for now. No need to be *too* ambitious).

I folded back a page of my legal pad and with my favorite pen (the uniball Signo 207 Impact 1.0mm point) I divided the page vertically into column "A," the *success* list, and column "B," the *happiness* list. First up: success.

This one's easy: my townhouse. Surely buying a home, on my own, in California, Los Angeles specifically, is an accomplishment that signifies success. I'm an official property owner! Excellent. Off to a great start. Next: happiness.

Okay...Let's see. Well, my townhouse makes me happy—it's my home, security, and, someday, my retirement fund. Okay, I can double up on that one.

Back to success... Hmm, lemme think, what else? Oh, I know, how about my MFA? I completed the program while working full time, going through a divorce, and in my fifties, no less. Shouldn't I chalk that up as a success, showing I can accomplish anything I put my mind to...? Not really. Sure, it's a master's degree, but it's a liberal arts master's degree. In my neighborhood, that and ten dollars'll get you a handjob. Wait! There you go: that's something to be happy about.

So I wrote it down and reviewed my lists:

Success

- My townhouse

Happiness

- My townhouse.
- $10 handies right outside my front door.

.

.

.

That was it.

I stared at the page wracking my brain for another line item.

There must be something I have in my life that makes me feel successful, happy, or loved.

I thought it over some more.

How about my health? That's always a strong indicator of success and happiness. True, but I'm a clinically depressed fifty-six-year-old man with high cholesterol, hypertension, and a brain tumor.

Ugh. Next...?

How about finances—that's a reliable go-to for defining success. It is but I'm a financially over-extended fifty-six-year-old man with student debt, little savings, and a low credit score.

Strike two. The windup and the pitch...

How about love? I have my family and friends. And like the Wizard of Oz told the Tinman, "A heart is not judged by how much you love, but by how much you are loved by others."

Yeah, but my closest friends are 400 miles away, and I never see them. My brothers are even farther away, and I never see them either. My dad's dead, my mom's dead, my cat's dead, and my marriage is dead. Plus, now that I read it again, that Wizard's quote is really just a buncha nonsense circular logic bullshit. Why the fuck am I even listening to that idiot anyway. He was a fake, a fraud, a charlatan. Fuck that guy. And nix family and friends.

Game and match. The only thing I seemed to be successful at

was convincing myself I wasn't successful—and I didn't feel very happy or loved doing it.

Totally rejected, I returned to my childhood cereal commercials, Peanut Butter Cap'n Crunch, and binging on *Mad Men*.

The Don Draper Formula for Success: Meet Dick Whitman

For the uninitiated, *Mad Men* is a TV show set in the 1960s about rich, entitled, good-looking Caucasians who have "everything" yet are never satisfied with their success, ultimately unhappy with their lives, and restlessly seek sex outside their marriages as a replacement for true love lost (or never was).

The lead character—*SPOILER ALERT!*—Midwestern farm boy Dick Whitman reinvented himself as handsome, suave, alcoholic advertising man Donald Draper to achieve everything everyone needs to be successful, happy, and in love: a prestigious career, plenty of money, a large home in the well-to-do suburbs, a beautiful wife, unlimited extramarital sex, happy, healthy children, and privilege beyond privilege.

Yet, he wasn't happy.

As I watched the umpteenth episode of *Mad Men* (I freakin' love that show) I was struck with how Don Draper's perfect life was built off a blueprint he didn't draft. Despite having the career he wanted, he'd play hooky from work, sometimes for weeks at a time, just to escape the very life he had created. He didn't value money so that didn't move his happiness needle. And he considered his perfect wife and children an encumbrance (really—one time he skipped out on his daughter's sixth birthday party and drove to a vacant lot where he sat alone in his car, smoking and thinking about... God knows what).

The person he *actually* was, Dick Whitman, found his happiness in simpler things; working on cars, traveling to new places without purpose, and a small, modest West Coast oceanside house with his platonic friend Anna. There and with her, Dick didn't need alcohol or sex to fill his pit of discontent. There, he was himself... successful, happy, and loving.

An Attitude of Gratitude

There's an old saying that goes: *I cried because I had no pants until I met a man who wore bell bottoms.*

Roughly translated, this means no matter how bad you have it, there's always some other poor bastard who's more fucked than you.

At that moment... for one single second... I deviated from my narrative of success, happiness, and love unjustly denied to a more rightsized perspective that, as bad as it was for me, it could've been a lot worse.

I lost my job because of the deadliest worldwide pandemic since the Great Influenza of 1918. And that is a tragedy. (Well, both are a tragedy.) But I never really liked my job very much. I took it to pay the bills—which it did. I was always appreciative, but never inspired. And why was that? The answer surprised me. *Because I never thought I had the right to be.*

A job is a job. It's not supposed to inspire me—that's why it's a job.

"Everyone" hates their job—but they do it anyway. Where do I get off thinking I should be any different?

At this point, I want to interject that I wasn't questioning the fact that I needed a job to pay my bills. Of course I did (as I do now). What I *was* challenging was how I formed a core belief that something I spent the vast majority of my waking hours doing five out of seven days a week, month after month, year after year, decade after decade could be something I didn't enjoy doing.

The first answer that popped into my head was... *money. I need money to pay my bills.* But I also needed enough left over to allow myself the creature comforts that made me feel successful and happy.

Like what?

Well, while I didn't take a detailed accounting of my monthly expenditures, I do remember hoping that whatever I was spending my money on was making me happier than what I was doing to make it.

And that sent me on an inward spiral, questioning everything I valued, pursued, and obtained. But more important than the *what* was the *why?*

Why did the things I pursued to make myself successful, happy, and loved make me so miserable when they were gone?

No. That's not it.

Why did I believe *those* things would make me successful, happy, and loved?

Closer.

Why would I allow things that could be taken away from me without my consent form the foundation of my personal success, happiness, and love?

Disco.

I began to reframe what I had lost and how it made me feel...

A job can be important to me to have and to keep but not the deciding vote of whether I'm a failure or not.

Financial security can make me happy (and it does), but it need not be the only thing that gives me happiness.

A relationship (romantic or platonic) can be the way I express love and am loved but it's not the ultimate factor in whether I'm worth loving.

If Don Draper was sold a fake bill of goods, then maybe I was too. If Dick Whitman could be happy with the most basic of life's blessings in disguise, then maybe I could too. This led me to my second epiphany: ***I've been driving someone else's car.***

I left the cruise control on for *way* too long and by the time the crappy music woke me up I'd been driving aimlessly for three years. All I wanted to know was:

1. **Who sold me this lemon?**
2. **Can I trade it in for a better model?**

Eventually, the process resulting from those two questions provided these two answers, respectively:

1. **People who prioritized their own interests and agendas.**
2. **I don't need to.**

Because a car seat is moveable, the steering wheel tiltable, the mirrors adjustable, the radio stations changeable, and the pine tree air freshener throwawayable, we don't have to conform to someone else's car. We can make modifications for a custom fit. Which steers us right into epiphany three.

CHAPTER 6

EPIPHANY THREE...

Genuine epiphanies are extremely rare... It is usually only in dramatic representations, religious iconography, and the 'magical thinking' of children that insight is compressed to a sudden blinding flash.
—David Foster Wallace

The guy wrote a 978-page novel with 98 pages of endnotes. I'm sure the compressing of anything's inconceivable to him.
—M.K. Jackson

E piphany three.
        The third epiphany.
It's the one that—
Shit... I'm drawing a blank...
Well, this is embarrassing.
I forgot epiphany three.
I know I had a third one. It was one of the three reasons I wrote this book. And I *know* I had *three* of them because I like grouping things in threes (and fives, and tens)
What the hell was it...?
Tell you what: when I remember, I'll come back to it and share it with you.
So, I guess we'll just move on to chapter 7.

CHAPTER 7
MAKE IT A RULE TO VALUE YOUR BELIEFS

The trouble with having an open mind, of course, is that people will insist on coming along and trying to put things in it.
—Terry Pratchett

And that is exactly why I deliberately remain closed-minded.
—M.K. Jackson

When I grow up, I wish I had become a lawyer. They're like magicians.* Using verbal misdirection and semantic smoke and mirrors logic, a good lawyer can transform a golden sponge cake with creamy lard filling into a legal murder defense, PMS into a valid reason for stabbing a co-worker to death, and, in a show-stopping feat of responsibility-vanishing rationale, make hot coffee *too* hot.

They do this by peeling Silly Putty off the fine print revealing a reversal of logic which they then stretch and twist into a dialectic pretzel to mean whatever the hell they want it to mean.

---

* I also contemplated becoming a magician in my ninth through thirteenth years—until I discovered girls and was told in no uncertain terms that guys, cut from the same rainbow-bedazzled, unicorn-emblazoned, denim bib-and-brace overalls cloth as Doug Henning who practice magic are unlikely to also practice kissing.

In legal prestidigitation, there's a big difference between *innocent* and *not guilty*.

When it comes to creating success, happiness, and yes, even love in our own lives, we can learn a lot from these wily wranglers of jurisprudence. By adopting a lawyerly approach, we can reshape our rules, values, and beliefs so they define success, happiness, and love in any way we want them to.

Circumnavigating Your Rules, Values, and Beliefs

A ship uses a compass to navigate its way; an airplane a heading indicator; and a car, GPS. Without these directional devices, each of these modes of transport would wander aimlessly, possibly never arriving at their desired destination. Likewise, to navigate our way through the challenges and obstacles of our lives, we human beings use our **rules, values, and beliefs.** These are the three filters through which we evaluate virtually everything we think, say, and do.

Should your career choice be based more on personal fulfillment rather than financial gain—or is money your focus while you tolerate the situation?

Did you choose your life partner because of the way you see them or because of the way you see yourself when you're with them? Or *both*?

Do you drive the speed limit even though there is no one else on the road?

Will you tell a little white lie if it gets you out of an embarrassing situation?

Did you decide to finish your work rather than go to the movies or did you blow off your work to go to the movies?

All of these situations and decisions are products of your rules, values, and beliefs.

You even chose to read this book based on your rules, values, and beliefs—after I decided to write it based on *my* rules, values, and beliefs.

Given the power these guiding principles have over us, it's of paramount importance that we ask ourselves three questions:

1. What the hell are they?
2. Where did they come from?
3. Are they best serving my success, happiness, and love?

If you don't know the answers to those questions—or the answers are not in *your* best interest—you're likely flying blind with no idea just how far off course you have likely drifted.

The ABCs of RVBs (Rules, Values, and Beliefs)

At first thought, rules, values, and beliefs may seem to be the same thing. While there is certainly some overlap, they are actually quite distinct from one another and originate from disparate sources in our lives (which, as we shall soon see, can be problematic). In addition, different people may have vastly different rules, values, and beliefs regarding the same things. To get us all on the same page, rules, values, and beliefs as they will be discussed in this book are defined thusly:

Rules are absolute. They rarely, if ever, change and leave little to no room for interpretation.

There are four main types of rules:

Societal—Social mores. The (sometimes unwritten) dictates of acceptable behavior in society such as *first come first served, don't interrupt someone while they're talking* (wait until they take a breath *then* interrupt them), and *wait your turn*. Generally speaking, these types of rules are not enforceable by law but are nevertheless followed as a means of inclusion within a community.

Regulatory—Commonly realized in the form of *laws, bylaws,* and *regulation*s. Violating these rules normally results in punish-

ment—school expulsions, workplace firings, fines, parking cita-
tions, community service, traffic tickets, arrest, and jail/prison.

Religious/Spiritual—Religion, spirituality, and especially
cults are nothing *but* rules. And to make it more complex and
restrictive, different religions/groups/cults have their own rules
which often contradict the others'.

Thou shall not kill (unless God sanctions it), *Keep holy the
Sabbath day. Truth is eternal. Love your neighbor as yourself* (the
"*Golden Rule*"). *Don't smoke dope. Do smoke dope. Don't have sex.
Do have but sex only in wedlock. Don't have sex in wedlock if you're
wedlocked to another person. Have sex* instead *of being wedlocked.
Masturbate. Don't masturbate. Do masturbate but only instead of
having sex when you are wedlocked. Don't masturbate in wedlock if
the person you're thinking about is wedlocked to somebody else.
Masturbate so you don't have to be wedlocked. Masturbate but only
to people you can't be wedlocked to. Masturbate while smoking dope
instead of having sex with your neighbor's wife (or husband).* The
list is Goddamn endless. (Oh, and *don't take the Lord's name in
vain.*)

Growing up, I witnessed firsthand the clash over liturgical
dogma between my mom (Catholic) and dad (Protestant)
concerning the most profound theological doctrines such as
dietary matters. For example, my dad wanted round stake on
Friday after work. My mom had to explain Lent to him. He had
to explain that the pope didn't pay our grocery bills to her. My
mom had to explain hell to him. He had to explain bullshit like
"hell" is why there's Protestantism. She had to explain to him
that Catholicism is why there's Protestantism. And it would go
on like that for, oh, I dunno, eighteen years until my mom
explained to my dad the inner and outer peace that comes with
converting to Catholicism. You get the point.

SIDE NOTE: Raised Catholic, "celebrating Palm Sunday"
was the first sin I ever committed that could've landed me in
hell. It was devastating to a young boy of twelve, planting (or
spilling) the seeds of guilt and self-loathing, leading to my

perception later in life that masturbation is revenge sex against myself. *Thanks, Catholic Church!*

Personal—Rules we hold individually and apply to ourselves (*my word is my bond, no more adultery this month*) and enforce upon others (*shoes off in my house, no one uses my gun*, and *last one there is a rotten egg*). What sets these rules apart from the other categories is that their sole purpose is to benefit (or hinder) us. While we may enforce them upon others (*my house, my rules*), we don't care whether others hold or embrace these rules for themselves—so long as they follow them for us. Personal rules can be healthy for our development if designed from the necessity to realize something advantageous *or* they can be detrimental if we adopt them, no questions asked, from others and they run contradictory to our best interests.

Values are our most deeply held ideals—our principles. Based on ethics and morals, values shape our character and define who we are as a person. They establish our standards of behavior and personal code of conduct. Frequently, values can be stated in a single word, such as *honesty, manipulation, compassion, greed, responsibility, respect, integrity, self-reliance* (hyphenated, but technically one word), *courage, duplicitous*, and *loyalty*.

Values are not so much taught as they are *introduced* to us— especially at a very young age. They originate from a variety of sources including family, friends, community, media, and religion/spirituality.

Beliefs are contextual. They are ideas *you* hold to be true. We embrace our beliefs as true without the necessity of proof—they are not universal truths. Beliefs are developed from many different sources including societal and cultural mores, religious/spiritual tenets, other people (usually authority figures such as parents, teachers, and role models), social organizations, and the media (movies, TV, music, books, etc.). You may believe *people are basically good* while someone else believes *people are basically bad*. Some believe *might is right*, others believe *violence is never an option*. Who's right? Who's wrong? Who cares? It's a belief!

"Big G" and the Pot Roast End

A product of *both* the Great Depression *and* World War II, my paternal grandmother, "Big G" (as my brothers and I came to call her), was a wise, self-assured, independent woman. From the moment I could understand language, she was filling my brain with nuggets of wisdom: *I never learned anything I didn't have to pay for... You never know when it's opportunity knocking, so you just have to keep answering the door... Save the principal, spend the interest...* and the one that's made the greatest impact on me to this day, *Trust no living man and walk carefully around the dead ones—* she taught me that when I was eight.

Her relentless barrage of dogmatic beliefs, moralizing narratives, unremitting lectures, and wholesale suspicions toward humanity made me the man I am today back when I was still a boy. However, as I grew older, I slowly began to realize much of what she sold me was in fact nicked from some intentionally uncredited source dressed up as her own life experiences. One such yarn was *The Pot Roast End*.

Big G told me she used to cook a pot roast by cutting off the end and placing it in the pot with the rest of the roast. When I took the bait and asked her why, she told me:

"It was how my mother taught me to do it when I was a little girl."

Okay.

After decades of unquestioning loyalty to this culinary custom, Big G finally asked her mother why it was necessary to cut the end of the pot roast. Was it something to do with flavor? Cooking time?

"I'm not sure," her mother told her. "It's how *my* mother taught me to cook a roast."

Not satisfied with that answer, Big G then approached her grandmother and asked:

"What's the reason you cut off the end of the roast to cook it? Is it something to do with cooking time or flavor or juices?"

"No," answered her grandmother. "My pot's too small for the roast. I cut off the end so it'll fit inside."

Apparently, my great, great grandmother had more meat than pot and for three generations her method was needlessly followed, always accepted, and never questioned.

Aside from the fact that this story firmly establishes the predisposition of the Jackson family to never question instructions from authority figures (making us ideal marks for cult leaders and fascists), it perfectly illustrates how behaviors as adults are often the consequences of residual, irrelevant programming from childhood, validating why we *must* be aware when deleteriously cutting off the end of our pot roast.

The Origin Story of Rules, Values, and Beliefs

Our rules, values, and beliefs are a cock block of heterogeneous viewpoints, randomly instilled (or *installed*) in us primarily during our formative years by people and institutions claiming they know what's best for us. To be fair, some do. But others are imposing their own rules, values, and beliefs on us to manage how we behave in service to their agendas—and that's where it gets tricky.

Truth is, it doesn't matter whether their intentions were/are benevolent or nefarious. Even the most positive rules, values, and beliefs we've acquired can be conflicting, contradicting, and irreconcilable with our success, happiness, and love when they lack continuity and a singular purpose, *our* purpose.

Let me ask you something: as an adult, how did you settle on your rules, values, and beliefs? Was it through years of careful consideration, experiential observation, and exhaustive imple-mentation? I'm willing to bet "no," "no," and "no." The scary truth of it is we have very little to do with shaping our initial rules, values, and beliefs (which is why I make it a rule not to value my beliefs).

So, what then is the origin story of our rules, values, and beliefs? They're most often formed in our earliest years by others in a position of influence over us. Throughout our lives, begin-ning when we're young and impressionable, there are people and institutions in our lives that have a stake in shaping our rules, values, and beliefs—some well-meaning, some not. They include:

- parents
- other family members
- friends
- school
- religion/church/spirituality
- political parties
- the media
- heroes and idols
- The Establishment (AKA "The Man")

Looking at that list, what would you guess they all have in common? I'll give you a hint: it's what they *don't* have in common: *you*. The answer is that *each one has its own agenda*. Not only are they indifferent to whether their agenda conflicts with one another's, some of them don't even care if their agenda conflicts with *yours*.

When you were five years old you knew cigarettes were bad for you. It probably wasn't the result of a dialectical conclusion formulated by negative experiences you had smoking compared and contrasted to data obtained by the scientific method. It's more likely someone *told* you cigarettes were bad for you. (But only if you were a kid *after* the 1970s. Otherwise, you probably got a carton of them in your Christmas stocking every year like I did.) My guess is you were warned to lay off the smokes by someone with a vested interest in your health. Someone who was an authority figure in your life or otherwise held sway over you such as a parent, a friend, or a medical professional. Of course, in some cases programming a child *not* to smoke is arguably a good thing. But what about when the motives are less benevolent?

In the 1930s, 40s, and 50s, children were encouraged to smoke by Santa Claus himself, lighting up in ads for no fewer than ten cigarette companies.* If you were a child in the late 1980s, Camel was at it again, appealing to your repchildrenian brain by using a cartoon character named Joe Camel. *Cartoons > fun > breakfast cereal > candy > toys > cigarettes!* Not all rules, values, and beliefs installed in us by people and institutions in our lives have *our* best interests in mind.

Let's say, as a child, you were given strict religious rules that prohibited recreational sex, illicit drug use, and tattoos. Yet, when you attended college, you were exposed to the value of questioning authority and the belief that exploring the boundaries of sex, consciousness, and tattoos enriched your insight into the human experience. So naturally, the idea of an ayahuasca weekend sounded intriguing. *But that's their religion*, a voice in your head mandated, *not yours*. So you reluctantly, yet willingly (???), remained behind in the dorm with all the other adherents, joyless and resentful of the Bible. This massive cluster fuck raged between your rules, values, and beliefs leading to guilt, shame, and alienation. You graduated a virgin, emotionally stunted, and socially awkward. Unemployable, you wound up as a jobbing, conflicted tattoo artist, your only meaningful physical contact with other humans is the needle with which you cause them pain.

---

* You know who you are, Camel, Chesterfields, Lucky Strike, Marlboro, Old Golds, Pall Mall, Parliament, Phillip Morris, Salem, and Winston.

That's the power of rules, values, and beliefs.

Childhood Constrict, Adulthood Conflict

When we're young our brain is especially elastic. But as we age, it *snaps* more than it *stretches* and so much of that childhood programming remains with us into adulthood. Therefore, like so many other childhood traumas, this programming anchors our rules, values, and beliefs while dangerously going unseen, unchallenged, and unchanged.

It's discouraging that so many significant aspects of our psyche were given to us like a Quick Pick lottery ticket and the only thing we can do is cross our fingers and hope it pays out in our favor. Unfortunately, it rarely does. Using the rules, values, and beliefs of *others* to filter and evaluate decisions for *our* success, happiness, and love, conflicts are going to arise.

Let's say you *value* creativity and desire a career in the arts. But, you also *believe* it to be a frivolous pursuit that ends only in poverty. CONFLICT! Whether you choose a creative career to fulfill your soul or one in business to ensure steady, gainful employment, you'll be neither successful nor happy in either career path, forced to live a hollow shell of a life filled to capacity with misery and failure. Thank your values and beliefs.

Perhaps you make it a *rule* to never use online dating because you *value* genuine human interaction, and you *believe* the internet is a modern-day Sodom and Gomorrah roadshow full of narcissists, liars, predators, and perverts lurking behind every URL making you just one right swipe away from hooking up with a nickel bopper on the prowl looking to lure a fornicatrix to their cyber peanut butter party for a little prostidigitation. CONFLICT! CONFLICT! CONFLICT! Your rules, values, and beliefs have eliminated, for you, the number one method people employ for amorous adventures: online dating sites. Your chances of finding a soulmate for life are infinitely more difficult; some would say impossible. You will likely die alone.

As you can see from these two real-life examples, CONFLICTS! between your rules, values, and beliefs can be a real pisser—let alone insurmountable obstacles to your success, happiness, and love. But fear not, there *is* hope…

Wash that Brainwash Right Out of Your Brain

You may believe that by the time you become an adult, with all your experiences, lessons learned, and time served, you're now forming your own rules, values, and beliefs. If this were true, grownups would have all the answers. But it's not and they don't.

While those aforementioned traits of age do contribute to an adult evaluation process the problem is the basis of that evaluation is the residual corrupt programming from your childhood. So, when making evaluations as an adult, you are, in essence, making a shitty Xerox, of a shitty Xerox, of a shitty Xerox.

This is why a total reprogramming from root to fruit is required—and, as you will discover while making your way through this book, is a matter of reverse engineering by beginning with the desired end result: your success, happiness, and love.

Expanding upon our previous example, let's say you pursue a creative career—musician, artist, actor, writer, cobbler, whatever coats your throat. *How* will you define your success in that field? This is a VERY important question, one that few people ponder before leaping from the frying pan into a career, relationship, or other no-win scenario.

Say you have a *rule* that career success is defined by being *paid* to do it. Problem is you aren't being paid to do it. So eventually, you quit. Now you have no income *and* you're not doing the thing you love and value in your life. *Great job!* No matter what you do, you are now perfectly set up for failure. And *that* is the naked, merciless power of rules, values, and beliefs.

For years, I considered my biggest failure in life to be my

divorce. But I now have a better relationship with my ex-wife than I did when we were married. We even sheltered in place together during the pandemic for two years while a divorced couple without one single argument. We continue to build mutual love and respect, communicate better, and set healthier boundaries than we did when married. Of course, everyone I tell this to, including my friends, thinks I'm nuts. And I am nuts— like jam-packed in both squirrel's cheeks nuts. BUT, I'm also now successful and happy in that relationship. All it took to see the success of our relationship and be happy with it was redefining my destructive rules, values, and beliefs which made me see it as a failure.

I spend a fuckload of my precious few days left here on earth writing. Yet, I make no income from it (and being just a third of the way through this book, I'm sure you see why). BUT, I *value* creativity in my life. I *believe* creating is an expression of the divine spark in each of us. And so I make it a *rule* that as long as I'm doing something creative and enjoying it—compensated or not—I'm successful at it. And that makes me happy. Sure, I'd love to make an income from it, but not at the cost of giving it up just because it isn't lucrative. (Besides, that's what multi-level marketing is for.)

Returning to the transportation analogy, imagine your life as a train. A train is different than a plane, a ship, or a car. It doesn't require a compass, heading indicator, or map to find its way to its destination because it travels on fixed tracks (rules, values, and beliefs). But what if those tracks lead you to an undesired destination? You board a train in Los Angeles for Chicago, but the tracks lead to Seattle. As wonderful as Seattle may be, Chicago is where you want to be. No matter how many times you travel that track, the train will never take you where you want to be.

That is unless you choose—or build—a different track.

CHAPTER 8
WHEN LIFE GIVES YOU LEMONS, MAKE WHISKEY SOURS

Life has become immeasurably better since I have been forced to stop taking it seriously.
—Hunter S. Thompson

I'm sure for Dr. Thompson, a native son of Louisville, Kentucky, life also lost its seriousness when taking it with whiskey—Chivas Regal in particular. It's true for me—except with Woodford Reserve.
—M.K. Jackson

The best works of science fiction predict the future (*Planet of the Apes*), introduce us to astounding new gadgets (*Star Wars*), dictate fashion (*Lost in Space*), and comment on human nature (*Manimal*). But *Star Trek* did all that and *more*. It commented on our current times while predicting the shape of things to come through life in the twenty-third century. From *Star Trek*, we got flip phones (technology), that poor bastard in the red shirt who's always the first one killed (fashion), Mr. Spock getting some trim once every seven years (sex, relationships & marriage), and the single greatest life success formula ever of all time: *The Kobayashi Maru*.

Introduced in the 1982 film *Star Trek II: The Wrath of Kahn*, The Kobayashi Maru is both the name of a civilian star freighter and a Starfleet Academy training exercise. In the simulation, a distress call is received by a Federation starship from the Kobayashi Maru. Having been disabled by a gravitic mine, the freighter is now a sitting duck at the mercy of the dastardly Klingons. Rushing to the aid of the Kobayashi Maru will provoke a Klingon attack, resulting in certain death for the Federation starship's crew. On the other hand, taking no action means annihilation for the Kobayashi Maru and all those aboard at the hands of the Klingons.

The test was designed to be a *no-win scenario*. Its purpose is to reveal the candidate's character, leadership skills, decision-making process, confidence, and poise under the insurmountable realization that, as a direct result of their actions (and inactions), people will die. So, of course, no cadet in the history of the Starfleet Academy had ever successfully bested the Kobayashi Maru—that is, no one except then-cadet *James T. Fucking Kirk*.

But it's *how* Kirk beat The Kobayashi Maru's no-win scenario that makes it relevant to this book. As Kirk himself explained it...

"I reprogrammed the simulation, so it was possible to rescue the ship... I changed the conditions of the test. Got a commendation for original thinking. I don't like to lose... I don't believe in the no-win scenario."[1]

Holy fuck—this guy's *awesome*! Kirk changed the rules to *his* advantage. He was like, *fuck this. I'm not letting some stupid test determine whether or not I become a Starfleet captain and get my own TV show in color. Goddamnit, I'm the one in control of my success, happiness, and love with green alien women.*

In other words, Kirk couldn't control the wind, so he adjusted the sails.

Even though most of us are not twenty-third-century space cadets beaming down to alien worlds and battling Klingons, we're still faced with our own twenty-first-century "no-win scenarios" especially when it comes to success, happiness, and love. And when we succumb to the parameters and restrictions of these situations, we're also at the mercy of their outcomes—and they rarely align in our favor.

Kobayashing *Your* Maru

In preparation for Kobayashing *your* Maru, let's review the *Five Takeaways from James T. Kirk and the Kobayashi Maru.*

1. We need not determine nor define our success and happiness using scenarios (rules, values, and beliefs) created by other people and institutions.

His refusal to believe in a no-win scenario is what motivated Cadet Kirk to rejigger the Kobayashi Maru's schemo. Because the scenario didn't work to his benefit in Kirk's mind it was defective and had to be redressed.

The same is true for us when our rules, values, and beliefs are a detriment to our success, happiness, and love. So, like Cadet Kirk, we reprogram—*THATS IT! I JUST REMEMBERED THE THIRD EPIPHANY! When I wrote* "success, happiness, *and* love," *it jogged my memory **because the order is wrong!** It's not* success, happiness, *and love; it's* happiness *THEN* success *and love. THAT was the third epiphany...*

EPIPHANY THREE: DON'T PUT THE SUCCESS CART BEFORE THE HAPPINESS HORSE

(CHAPTER 6B)

Believe me, this digression back to epiphany three will be worth it!

The general wisdom shoveled at us while growing up was that being successful makes you happy. But personal experience has now led me to believe that's not wisdom, it's wisdumb.

From what I've experienced it's actually the other way around. Being happy is what leads to being and *feeling* successful. And *that* was my third and final epiphany that inspired me to write this book: *never put the success cart before the happiness horse.*

After my life cratered, I found myself in a paradoxical conundrum: I was unhappy because I was unsuccessful. I thought to be happy (again) I had to be successful (again). But I was so unhappy I had trouble getting out of bed in the morning. So how then could I grab the world by its salted nuts in the way necessary to regain my success?

When I thought about beginning the long and grueling climb back up Success Mountain once again, I immediately lost all interest in it. It was so much work and heartbreak the *first* time. So much in fact, I even began questioning the necessity of happiness.

Was being happy really worth all the trouble given *The Law of Diminishing Trying*? (See chapter four if you forgot what this is— or if you weren't really all that impressed with it the first time.)

After agonizing over this dilemma for several months, it hit me with the subtlety of a cast iron skillet in the face that usually in my life, when I have so much trouble with something— anything—it's because I'm fucking with the natural order of things—the definition of which, for my purposes is *the orderly system comprising the physical universe and functioning according to natural as distinguished from human or supernatural laws*[1].

As a control freak, I really like to... control things. But as I age and grow wiser (both of which do seem mutually exclusive for me) I better understand that things would much rather control themselves, without my will forced upon them. It's only in a Zen state of going with the flow that I can become *part of* what I'm experiencing rather than an *opponent of it*. It was in that vein/vain so began my lofty thoughts.

In the natural order of things, I wondered, does the "universe" (science, metaphysics, God, nature... whatever keeps one's boat afloat) deem it more natural/important/necessary that I am first and foremost *happy* or *successful*? Is one more vital than the other as a human in this being? Is one the doorway to the other? Is one more dispensable than the other? Because if one does lead to the other (even if only with a slight edge) then I better make sure I'm pursuing them in the correct *natural order*.

Like other preeminent philosophers, I'm great at asking questions, not so great at answering them. But thank deliciousness for my propensity to apply myself as little as possible for the least results required. Since I've always seen being successful as "work" and being happy as "enjoyable," I figured why not just eat dessert before dinner? That is, reverse the *success-first-then-happiness* modality so the *fun* part leads to the *hard* part. Seemed rational, doable, and EZ to me.

Knowing I'm less Lief Eriksson and more Christopher

Columbus (but, you know, without the torture, enslaving, and genocide), I figured any destination at which *my* thought process arrived must have a predecessor's flag already planted there. So, intending to ratify rather than claim my new route to success by way of happiness, I decided to consult a source far more enlightened than myself. A modern-day oracle possessing the sageness and knowledgness of the ages. A fountainhead with all the answers. I refer, of course, to the almighty god-fearing, god-forsaken, god-damned World Wide Web. So, I hopped on HotBot, launched Lycos, and asked Jeeves one simple question: *which comes first, happiness or success?*

The oracle's answers were swift and surprising. That virtually every answer was *happiness*—happiness comes first *then* success—was far less astonishing than the wells from whence they sprang. I mean, I figured I was onto something and was more than likely correct in my contention that we cannot experience fulfilling, lasting success without first imbued with true, unequivocal happiness. But I would have never guessed just *who* agrees with me on that. It wasn't just the usual feel-good-believe-it-then-you'll-see-it-make-a-vision-board suspects. Nay, the vast majority were *business* sources including *Inc.*, *Forbes*, and *Fast Company*(!) The very proponents of business-related success were emphatically in agreement that being happy *first* is imperative, even *required*, to be successful.

An online article in *Forbes* by Nick Bennett titled "The Secret Of Success - Is It Happiness?"[2] points out that "The path of success leading to happiness is baked into us from an early age. Yet neuroscience suggests we may have the sequence the wrong way round," noting that happiness makes the brain work better because it "...triggers the release of serotonin and dopamine, which significantly enhance motor control, motivation, memory, problem-solving, mental focus and the ability to process multiple concepts simultaneously." All necessary traits and states for success.

The more I searched, the more I discovered other capitalist sources asserting that success comes from happiness. It was like Cornelius explaining his finds at the archeological dig in the cave to Dr. Zaius at the end of the first and best *Planet of the Apes* movie:

"That's the paradox. For the more ancient culture is the more advanced."

An *Inc.com* article by Jeff Haden titled "A Surprising Truth About the Misunderstood Relationship Between Happiness and Success"[3] takes on the sophism that "hard work and sacrifice lead to success and happiness is the by-product." Citing a study published in *Psychological Bulletin* that reviewed over 200 happiness studies, the researchers discovered "...the characteristics related to positive affect include confidence, optimism, and self-efficacy; likability and positive (outlooks towards) others; sociability, activity, and energy; prosocial behavior; immunity and physical well-being; effective coping with challenge and stress; and originality and flexibility."

Whoa! That's a lot of psychobabble mumbo jumbo there, Sir Thinksalot. Essentially, the researchers in all their labyrinthine psychespeak concluded that happy people tend to be more successful for two reasons:

1. because of their positive moods, they have a greater likelihood of actively working toward new successes;
2. given their previous pleasant moods, happy people have over time built more skills and resources (than unhappy people) with which to achieve success.

And finally, in their article "Which comes first: happiness or success?"[4] *Fast Company* quotes a five-year research project in which three prominent psychologists, two from the Naval Postgraduate School and one from the University of Pennsylvania's Positive Psychology Center, set out to discover *which comes first, happiness or success*. After interviewing over one million employees, the researchers found that the happiest among the employees "had almost four times the number of award recognitions as those in the group with the lowest well-being scores... happiness is a measurable predictor of performance."

Many more business/success-focused media platforms extol the natural order of happiness-*then*-success including the *Wall Street Journal*, *Entrepreneur*, and *Linkedin*. Even *Success* magazine concedes that happiness precedes success—and *success* is *literally* the name of their magazine.

Actually, now that I read about all these articles again, I guess it's not like Cornelius at all. Business publications touting happiness as a requisite for success don't really have a whole lot in common with advanced past cultures, or a talking archeologist chimp lecturing a fanatically dogmatic orangutan. But, it *is* a *paradox*.

Having verified my "happiness first" pathway to success with such authoritative sources, I'm convinced I'm on the right track (enough to write a book about it). (Frankly, even if all those business/success publications didn't agree with me I still wouldn't have given two shits on a fourth down blitz and continued rhapsodizing my epiphanizing that it's truefilling happiness that leads to fulfilling success, not the other way around.) However, there are two problems in adopting my new natural order:

Now I have to change the order of the words in the book's subtitle from "success, happiness, love" to "happiness, success, and love." Given the artwork has already been finalized and uploaded, this could be expensive or even too late—I have to check with all the publishing and distribution companies. (Since you're reading the finished book, you already have the answer to this—I hope it worked out in my favor.)

Second, I now have to pore over everything I've already written and switch around the *success/happiness* word order to *happiness/success* in every instance it appears. (I guess the find/replace function would be greatly advantageous for this.

Imagine if I'd written this longhand on paper instead of with a computer—I'd be fucked.)

Don't worry about all that though. You have enough to do just reading the book. I'll take care of writing it.

Okay, with epiphany three delivered, let's return to chapter 8...

WHEN LIFE GIVES YOU LEMONS, MAKE WHISKEY SOURS (CONTINUED)

(CHAPTER 8B)

AUTHOR'S NOTE: The previous epiphany three *chapter addendum added more words than I expected to this book and pushed it over the publishing industry's total word count standards for non-fiction books. I had to compensate by cutting some words from* this *chapter, so we'll rejoin chapter 8 already in progress. But don't sweat it. With my verbose, repetitive writing style it's actually doing you a favor.*

...which intensified the situation for Kirk—and why it's so applicable here. Just follow the same steps and consider it *your* Constitution-class cruiser.

4. There is no such thing as a no-win scenario.

What James T. Kirk did NOT believe in and would NOT accept were situations he could not overcome, AKA "no-win scenarios." This is a superior belief to have—especially when said situations and scenarios are not of our making yet they do determine, validate, and measure *our* happiness and/or success.

5. We have the ability to *reprogram* that which defines our happiness and success.

Life's not seven-card stud, it's five-card draw. We *can* reshape the hand we're dealt.

Later on, in part two of this book, I'll take you step-by-step through the process of reprogramming your "no-win" scenario into a "hella-win" scenario.

But first, let's explore a few more tools you'll use...

CHAPTER 9
MEDIOCRE JOKER

Some are born great, some achieve greatness, and some have greatness thrust upon 'em.
   —William Shakespeare, *Twelfth Night* Act II, scene v

Some men are born mediocre, some men achieve mediocrity, and some men have mediocrity thrust upon them.
   —Joseph Heller, *Catch-22*

Wow. Appropriating a line from Shakespeare then swapping its theme of greatness for mediocrity is not only ballsy it's what this entire goddamn book is all about. Bravo Mr. Heller!
   —M.K. Jackson, apparently the *second*-best writer regarding mediocrity.

When I was a kid, I saw an episode of *The Brady Bunch* called "The Teeter-Totter Caper." (Contrary to the title, it was not about the heist of a teeter-totter.) In the story, the two youngest of the Brady brood, Bobby and Cindy, feel marginalized because their older brothers and sisters won't let them help fix a radio or paint a chair. So, to show everyone that "little kids can do something important," the two set out to break the world record for teeter-tottering: 124 consecutive hours. (Even from my childhood perspective, this seemed like a wildly dispropor-tionate reaction. *If you won't let us paint a chair, we'll set a world record*.)

As a young boy, after seeing the episode, I too wanted to do something exceptional and be important, just like Bobby and Cindy Brady. So, I sent away for a copy of the *Guinness Book of World Records* from the back page of one of my comic books. When it finally arrived, I leafed through every page of the thick volume (nearly four inches!) looking for just one world record I could break.

Aside from a nine-year-old child becoming the fattest man alive (1,069 pounds—buried in a piano case!), I was unable to find a single world record within those 608 pages that I had even the remotest possibility of breaking.

I would've probably felt a lot worse about my failure to become a record holder but for the fact that Bobby and Cindy Brady also failed to set *their* world record. After teeter-tottering for only like twelve hours, they fell asleep at the handles, killing their chance to be important and relegating themselves into history's dustbin of also-rans.

Looking back, I can now plainly see that my desire for adula-tion and immortality faaaaar exceeded my motivation, commit-ment, and ability to achieve it. Even as a child I was indolent—a "needs to apply himself" type. My report card marks were uniformly straight down the middle column "S" for satisfactory —never "O" for outstanding… but neither "I" for inadequate either.

I was too tall to be a forward on the basketball team, yet not good enough to be the first-string center. While I got *some* time on the court (with a pretty good shot percentage), I warmed the bench for the majority of my grade school hoops career.

I was never part of the "popular kids" clique, nor was I exiled to the group of outcasts. I did, however, possess one prosaic talent that set me apart from my childhood peers: I could draw. But even that was limited to a single-angle perspective of

Fred Flintstone—from his necktie up. Nevertheless, I became a freak-like curiosity to my classmates who marveled at the speed and accuracy with which I could whip out identical sketch after sketch of Bedrock's favorite son on command, like a trained chimp, right before their very eyes.

By every account, I was a middling mainstreamer, a milquetoast moderate mediocre joker. Like Bobby and Cindy Brady, I too fell asleep, not on the teeter-totter of triumph, but on the merry-go-round of mediocrity, aimlessly and repeatedly circling for the next five decades, never to grab the brass ring. (Note to self: check the *Guinness Book* and see if *that's* some sort of world record.) The entire time I handicapped my happiness, success, and love by lamenting the fact that I was destined to be nothing but ordinary. No world record. No fame. No glory. No exceptionalism in this American.

That assessment remained my accepted lot in life for the rest of my early school years, through adolescence, past young adulthood, and into middle adulthood. Knowing I was mediocre I presumed only the lower tiers of happiness, success, and love were attainable to me because no matter how hard I tried, I could not escape my mediocrity. But what I didn't know at the time was neither could everyone else in the world.

It wasn't until a half-century into my life that I was finally able to recognize mediocrity NOT as a limitation to my happiness, success, and love, but as the pathway to it. And how did I finally get my jejune on and come to terms with being mediocre? What, you please must ask or I can't continue writing this book, was The Big Breakthrough? Well, there were actually *two*.

The Very Definition of Mediocre

No one likes to think of themselves as mediocre. This is due in large part to the efforts of the vast self-help conspiracy. Their deceptive etymological smear campaign has iniquitously given the word *mediocre* inaccurately negative connotations.

Of course, their motives are transparent. The self-help industrial complex could never sell its books, blogs, seminars, webinars, courses, and coaching without the specter of mediocrity looming over people's insecurities. The dissemination of these false narratives and defamatory accusations are contrived to prevent people from knowing the truth about mediocrity: by its very definition, *mediocre* really ain't all that bad. Don't believe me? Let's take a look...

mediocre

adjective

: *of moderate or low quality, value, ability, or performance: ordinary, so-so*[1]

To defang this big bad word, let's dismantle its definition. Note it clearly states that for something to be mediocre, the quality, value, ability, and performance must be moderate *or* low quality. Most important is the word *or*, the definition of which is *a conjunction used to link alternatives.*[2] In turn, the word *alternative* is defined as *two things mutually exclusive so that if one is chosen the other must be rejected.*[3] So we have the option to define our personal brand of mediocrity as moderate *or* low in quality. Always take the *moderate* road.

For the record I wish to state that low-quality mediocrity does have its place (just ask any politician). After all, not everything we do is worth doing moderately. For some things, low-level mediocrity is best (just ask any politician). But throttling down your efforts to sub-moderate should be reserved only for things that are *not* essential to success and happiness (just ask any politician). For everything else use *moderate*. Moderate is *keeping within reasonable or proper limits; not extreme, excessive, or intense.*[4] Do you know who was extreme, excessive, and intense without proper limits? Hitler. That's who. And look how he ended up: suicide pact with his new wife of one day on their honeymoon in a stuffy underground bunker. If that's not the epitome of unhappy, unsuccessful, and unloved I don't know what is. And I think we can all agree *moderation* is a good thing;

eating in moderation, smoking in moderation, alcohol in moderation, cocaine in moderation, even moderation in moderation.

But it's the last part of the definition, *ordinary, so-so*, that detractors of mediocrity cite as an affront to our "unlimited potential" (that we don't really have) to accomplish "extraordinary things" (that we'll never really do). We think *if I'm ordinary and so-so, how will I change the world?* Please, let me remove this Sisyphean burden from your shoulders right here and now. No one's asking you to change the world. The world's been around for 4.543 billion years and no one's been able to change it yet so what makes you think you can? And truth be told, the world doesn't want to change so you got a hard slog to hoe. Instead, I suggest you try another tact. Gandhi said, "Be the change that you wish to see in the world."* Now, *that's* much easier. Unless of course, you'd rather pattern your life on Hitler than Gandhi. Personally, I'm going with the Mahatma. But that's just me.

Still not sold on the merits of mediocrity? Not ready to release yourself from the specious shackles of unlimited potential?

What if I told you that your reluctance to embrace all that is mediocre within you runs counter to the law of nature and is in direct opposition to the evolutionary development of every life form throughout the entire God-forsaken Universe? Well, it is. And there's a scientific/philosophical/statistical theory that says so.

. . .

---

* Actually, that quote is not from Gandhi. It's from educator Arleen Lorrance. In the early 1970s Lorrance was a teacher at Thomas Jefferson High School in Brooklyn. She started The Love Project to improve the lives and education of the students at the school. The quote was first used in a report about the project, then later in a chapter she wrote for a 1974 book. Somehow, the Mahatma wound up getting credit for Ms. Lorrance's wise words. See? Even the woman who tried to change the world by making up a quote about changing the world isn't acknowledge for any change there may have been from her quote. Goddamn patriarchy.

The Mediocrity Principle

Did you know mediocrity has its very own principle? I didn't. And I consider myself an expert in all things mediocre.

Going way back in time to the works of Nicolaus Copernicus (1473-1543), scientists have recognized the mediocrity principle. And going way the hell back in time to when I began writing this book, I reckoned there was some sort of mediocre force in the cosmos imposing its unexceptional ascendancy over my life —I just didn't know it was a thing. But a thing it is and a thing it does.

In a nutshirt, the mediocrity principle asserts that the evolutionary process here on Earth that led to life and eventually "intelligent," "thinking" beings (us), is not unique and has likely been duplicated on sites throughout the cosmos. Consequently, there is nothing inherently special, exceptional, privileged, or even superior about we(e) humans. We are, by order of the universe/creation/gods/God, just another commonplace process that has occurred time and time again throughout the macrocosm.

Biologist and associate professor at the University of Minnesota, P.Z. Myers, explains it in more plain-ish speak:

The mediocrity principle simply states that you aren't special. The universe does not revolve around you, this planet isn't privileged in any unique way, your country is not the perfect product of divine destiny, your existence isn't the product of directed, intentional fate, and that tuna sandwich you had for lunch was not plotting to give you indigestion... the unique combination of traits that make you male or female, tall or short, brown-eyed or blue-eyed were the result of a chance shuffle of genetic attributes during meiosis, a few random mutations, and the luck of the draw in the grand sperm race at fertilization.[5]

Fuuuuuuuck.

Now, before you go and commit some Nietzschean act of surrender, understand this revelation is *not* bad news. Oh the contraire, it's *great* news. It means that all those times your buttinsky parents, teachers, significant others, and friends insensitively applied unbearable pressure on you by insisting that you could *do* better and *be* better, **they were wrong**. Every time they unfairly burdened you with presumptuous claims that you are special, extraordinary, or gifted, **they were wrong**. And if you're one of us poor bastards who's spent your life suffocating under the oppressive blanket of unlimited self-potential believing you're supposed to attain magnificence, **you were wrong**. Rejoice! You are now off the hook. Breathe a sigh of release and stop thinking of yourself as *unrealized excellence*. You aren't. None of us are. In fact, not only is our mediocrity baked into us cosmically, according to Professor Myers we're also random mutations from a shitty sperm race gone bad. If that doesn't give us all hope, I don't know what does.

Technically, the problem isn't that we're *not* good enough, it's that we're told we *are* good enough. Over and over and over and over. This has unjustly and unfairly inflated our sense of entitlement, which in turn elevates our expectations to a ridiculously unrealizable level. And once our chimerical exceptionality meets with the reality of our congenital mediocrity it's no wonder we feel as inadequate as an eight-year-old child desperately thumbing through the *Guinness Book of World Records* searching for something to be the best at.

We're told that if we work hard and save our pennies, we can be millionaires. In their speeches, Academy Award winners tell us *their* Oscar is proof that if we just work hard enough and believe in ourselves enough, we can accomplish anything. As kids our parents, teachers, and politicians tell us that we can be whatever we want to be when we grow up—even the president of the United States. And every child on the Little League diamond, Pop Warner gridiron, and youth basketball court is coached to believe that with lots of practice, they too can be just like their professional sports heroes.

That's all great talk and everything and it makes for rousing speeches and inspiring movies, but the *reality* is a Skin Bracer cold slap in the face…

- There are 47,000,000 millionaires in this world. That may seem like a lot but not when compared to the remaining 8,076,283,100 non-millionaires. That's a measly 0.581 percent of the entire world's population banking seven digits. Meanwhile, more than *half* of all adults worldwide have a net worth below $10,000.[6]
- Of the 439 films released in the United States in 2021,[7] only twelve of them received an Oscar at the 94th Academy Awards in March 2022[8]—that's only 2.7 percent of the films that were given the prestigious award. And there were a lot more films made than were officially released.
- Between the years 1780 and 2010, 305,365,169 people were born in the United States of America,[9] the greatest goddamned country in the history of the goddamned universe times infinity. From 1783 when George Washington was elected the first U.S. president to the 2020 election, just *forty-six people* (all men, all but one Caucasian) served as POTUS. Of those remaining 305,365,123 people, there's no way *every single one of them* could've been president—no matter what their parents told them.
- Less than eleven per one hundred, about 10.5 percent, of NCAA senior male baseball players will get drafted by a Major League Baseball team.[10]
- The chance of making it onto the USA Olympic Swimming Team: 0.0013 percent.[11]
- The chances of being drafted by an NBA team out of college is 0.02 percent. The NFL is slightly higher at 0.03 percent.[12]

Thanks, I needed that.

You will *never* convince me that the people included on the short end of those percentages failed to become millionaires, Oscar winners, United States presidents, or Olympians/professional athletes solely because they did not work harder, dream bigger, believe in themselves more, set better goals, journal daily, or thanked God enough in their prayers. Ninety-eight to ninety-nine percent of us are simply not destined for greatness—and not because we didn't buy the right self-help book or failed to hire the best success coach.

At the age of five, I wanted to be a baseball player when I grew up (like my hero, Reggie Jackson!) but I ended up a baseball watcher. I made my first movie when I was twelve yet I still don't have my Oscar. And I was never president of the United States so instead I had to settle for voting for them.

However, I did join a bowling team and we won first place in the league tournament. Several films I made won festival awards. And I was elected president of my homeowners association.

I readily acknowledge with adulatory pride that these achievements are of supreme mediocrity. But you know what? They are never the less *achievements*. And I know for damn sure I would have never accomplished *anything* had I aimed for those absurdly unattainable counterparts I listed in the paragraph preceding them. By lowering my sights and settling for ordinary, so-so objectives instead of going on some wild goose chase for "excellence," not only am I happy *and* successful sooner but I also have time left over to polish off all nine seasons of *Suits*.

Unleash Your Mediocre Joker

Hopefully, by now you're thinking *Wow, this mediocrity thing sounds really adequate—how do I get in on it?* The good news is mediocrity is not something we need to cultivate—it's our default. (From that shitty sperm race, remember?) Being mediocre is our cosmic birthright and endorsing it is an act of insurrectionary liberation.

In "The Teeter-Totter Caper" Cindy and Bobby thought they were better than everyone else *in the WORLD*. Teeming with hubris, they teeter-tottered too close to the sun and failed. They should've taken a cue from their older siblings, aimed lower, and say, *painted* the teeter-totter rather than try to set a world record with it. They didn't understand that with mediocrity you don't have to be *the* best, just *your* best. And that's okay because, at the end of the day, how many fattest men in the world can there really be? Only one. (And he was buried in a piano case!)

CHAPTER 10
THE FIVE OR SIX DESTRUCTIVE BELIEFS PREVENTING YOU FROM ACHIEVING HAPPINESS, SUCCESS, AND LOVE

He who believes he can and he who believes he can't are both usually right.
—Confucius

That guy sounds more confused than I am.
—M.K. Jackson

They come at you like thieves in the night cloaked in the erroneous belief that they are somehow contributing to your betterment. Under the guise of "just wanting to help you" or "it's for your own good" from well-meaning loved ones or success gurus with something to sell, these platitudes are the fountainhead of self-delusion, self-sabotage, and self-destruction. *Beware!*

They are *destructive beliefs*, and their only purpose is to give you false hope by making you believe you possess far more ability, ingenuity, talent, and wherewithal than you really do.

Shhhh... Listen... You can hear them contemptuously mocking you in the deepest recesses of your credulous mind...

You deserve better.

You can do anything once you put your mind to it.

You're so amazing, you could be with anyone you want.

Alas, the truth is that you do not necessarily *deserve* better. You cannot do *anything* once you put your mind to it. And you cannot have *anyone* you want. But you know what? Neither can 98 percent of the people on this planet (especially me).

Through my pioneering work in the field of *good enough*, I have identified *The Five or Six Destructive Beliefs Preventing You from Achieving Happiness, Success, and Yes, Even Love*. Why are they so dangerous? Well, think of them like weeds. If left untended they will take over your entire garden, strangle your beautiful plants, and kill off every possible chance you'll ever have for happiness, success, and love. Unfortunately, you have most likely adopted at least one, if not more, of these toxic tenets. Fortunately, this chapter will guide you through my *EZ Two-Step Process* for ripping these suckers out by the roots:

STEP 1: Identify the destructive belief(s). (Examples of which I will provide.)

STEP 2: Replace the destructive belief(s) with more realistic, limiting belief(s). (Examples of which I will provide.)

DESTRUCTIVE BELIEF #1: *I can do anything I put my mind to.*

The biggest problem with this belief is that it casts too wide a net. Look, I get it, you want to accomplish something great in your life. But rather than think you have to *accomplish something great*, think it's *great to accomplish something*. It's much easier to be happy and successful when you:

1. broaden your focus (don't set your sights on something too specific);
2. scale down (don't be too ambitious);
3. steer clear from things that are not in your wheelhouse (as the philosopher Harry Callahan wisely said, "A man's got to know his limitations." Works for all gender identities as well).

For example, say you want to climb Mount Everest. This *sounds* like an insurmountable goal because, oh, I don't know, maybe because *ninety-nine percent of the people on planet Earth can't do it!* So rather than traveling to the Himalayas in Nepal just to fail climbing Mount Everest, take your out-of-shape, never-even-seen-a-mountain ass to San Diego, California, and walk down *Mount Everest Boulevard*. It's paved, has a sidewalk, and is level so you can *definitely* conquer it. Technically it's not the mountain, but is there really any difference? No, not really. At the end of the day, you more or less accomplished what you wanted to do. Now you're successful, happy, and can wear an *I conquered Mount Everest* T-shirt.

USE THIS ALTERNATE BELIEF INSTEAD: *I'm not going to pressure myself into trying harder by thinking I'm better than I actually am.*

DESTRUCTIVE BELIEF #2: *A [gender identity] like me can have **any** [gender identity] I want.*

This belief is so far from reality it's comical. *Anyone*? Really? Your best friend's spouse? Your spouse's best friend? A movie star? Rock star? Supermodel? Professional athlete? The most important thing to remember with this one is **ALWAYS avoid absolutes**.

Look, it's okay if you never hook up with a movie star, rock star, supermodel, or athlete. Fact is, hooking up with one is a bad idea, to begin with. Do you know the odds against a successful celebrity marriage? Me neither. Not percentage-wise, anyway. But I do know it's not good. (Although you'd likely have double the chance of it succeeding since only half of you are a celebrity.) (But still, it's not a good idea.) Okay, so forget marriage, imagine the magnitude of the self-esteem-devastating competition playing at that level. Besides, if you're targeting a *kind* or *type*, it's probably not true love you're looking for anyway. (And frankly, if you're an ordinary someone who can hook up with a movie star, rock star, supermodel, or professional athlete, you shouldn't be reading this book; you should be writing your own.)

Meanwhile, back here on earth, never mind movie stars, rock stars, supermodels, and athletes, not even *every* "regular" person is available to you. For decades, I've obsessed over women in schoolrooms, workplaces, restaurants, grocery stores, churches, apartment buildings, shopping malls, stores in the shopping malls, adjacent parking spaces, buses, courtrooms, my condo, and on video cameras—often simultaneously but never successfully.

Remember the J. Geils Band song "Love Stinks?" *You love her, but she loves him, and he loves somebody else you just can't win.* That song is hella *true*. You have no control over who loves you, no matter how much you beg. The belief *you can have anyone you want* fails to acknowledge that love is not about *desire*, it's about *consent*. Who wants you is of greater consequence than who you want.

For those of you still struggling with this concept, I offer my quick start recovery guide to DLS (Delusional Love Syndrome)…

The Four Rules for Love in the Real World—**Valuable advice learned at the great personal expense of M.K. Jackson.**

1. Punch your weight.
2. Don't pursue those who don't want to be pursued.
3. Know what 100 yards looks like.
4. Understand that true love is *not* how the other person makes you feel about yourself, but *how you feel about the other person.*

Keep those rules in your front pocket and you'll avoid a butt-load of *fracas en el amor.*

USE THIS ALTERNATE BELIEF INSTEAD: *I don't need the one I want to need me, I just need to want the one who wants me.*

BONUS BELIEF: *Money can't buy love, but it can rent the next best thing for an hour or two.*

DESTRUCTIVE BELIEF #3: *I can accomplish* **anything** *if I just work hard enough.*

Again, with the absolutes. This is a variation on Destructive Belief #1 but different in that it attributes success to hard work alone, deceptively inferring that only people who work hard succeed. And who comes to a parochial conclusion like this? Yep, people who have succeeded. *The arrogance!* This dismissive, destructive belief leaves out all the other contributing factors to success covered in epiphany one—such as nepotism, timing, and just plain dumb luck).

There are an estimated 135,600 actors in the United States and only about fifty-seven of them (0.0420353 percent) are what we would recognize as "famous."[1] So for a movie star to say, "Just work hard, believe in your dreams, and you'll make it big like I did!" is disingenuous, delusional, and in denial of all other fortuitous factors that intervened in their success.

A *lot* of people work hard—construction workers, teachers, bus drivers, food servers, nurses, electricians, roofers, secretaries, gardeners, but they don't usually get rich and famous for it. But it doesn't mean they aren't successful at what they do or happy doing it.

USE THIS ALTERNATE BELIEF INSTEAD: *Without too much work I can accomplish anything I'm* **capable** *of accomplishing.*

DESTRUCTIVE BELIEF #4: *I am surrounded by supportive people who believe in me and want me to be happy and successful.*

Those aren't people, those are employees—and you have to pay them.

This destructive belief fosters the expectation that others will participate in your happiness and success. Some of them will, some of them won't, but none of them should—not in a negative way… or even in a positive one. Since you don't have control over the intentions or actions of others, the only one left you can completely rely on is *yourself*.

If you're ever to be genuinely happy, truly successful, or deeply loving in a lasting, meaningful, and authentic way, it must be completely immaterial to you whether someone else gives a crap (or not) about it. This is not a pessimistic view of humanity, it's an optimistic view of *your* self-empowerment. It's up to you and you alone to grab the bull by the balls and squeeze out all the happiness and success you can. (Just be sure the bull you're squeezing is *you*.)

USE THIS ALTERNATE BELIEF INSTEAD: *I believe in myself and want me to be happy, successful, and loving.*

DESTRUCTIVE BELIEF #5: *There is no such thing as failure…* followed by some nonsensical statement such as: *…as long as I learn from it* or *…because it contributes to me being better* or *…there's only a result,* and so on…

There's an old saying I just made up that goes like this: *If you fold your parachute incorrectly it won't open, and you'll hit the ground and you'll die.* Not much to learn from that failure except *you suck at folding parachutes and should stop doing it.*

Failing is not something that needs to be explained away, rationalized, or made excuses for. On the contrary, it should be embraced like a good friend who has the balls/ovaries to give it to you straight. Or even like a compass guiding you true north so you needn't needlessly wander the landscape of your life heading straight for *destination: futility.*

When I was on my grade school basketball team I was *just okay.* Not a starter, but not a benchwarmer either. I made the team, but I wasn't a go-to player in a clutch. I was *just okay.* So when the pressure was on us to rally from behind and win a game, the coach would *never* put me in—no matter how little time was left on the clock or what brief time I'd had on the court. That's because the stakes were too high and they didn't give out trophies for *just okay*.

As an adult, after I was laid off, I decided to shoot for the moon in my new job hunt. In a double-D-sized dual state of denial and delusion, I went after jobs I would've loved *doing* but wasn't even remotely *qualified* for. Sure, I *believed* I was—just like I once *believed* in Santa Claus, or voting for a particular politician would better my life. An assistant production manager at Paramount Pictures? Of course! I have two film degrees and made several movies when I was younger. (The haze of delusion was so dense, that I actually thought Paramount Pictures would hire film producers from a job posting on ZipRecruiter.) The deafening silence of *don't call us, we won't call you* that my résumé received woke me up to reality. I didn't get any interviews because they don't give out jobs for *unqualified*. This calls to mind my two favorite Bible quotes...

If a man's testicles are crushed or his penis is cut off, he may not be admitted to the assembly of the Lord.
   —Deuteronomy 23:1[2]

And ye shall know the mediocre and the mediocrity shall make you free.
   —John 8:32[3]

Both of these quotes remind us that if whatever we were trying to accomplish went wrong, we can pretty much guarantee it was doomed to fail because we bit off more than we could chew.

When I fail, rather than bucking intelligent design, I tamp down my expectations, lower my sights, and aim for the middle where I can chew every bit I bite and live happily and successfully ever after with my mouth comfortably full.

USE THIS ALTERNATE BELIEF INSTEAD: Failure is just God's way of telling me I'm not good enough.

This is not as negative as it may sound upon first reading (or as it may look upon first hearing). Only a person who is not confident in their mediocrity is concerned about failing. The rest of us understand this belief as the unbiased liberator it is.

What if someone asked you to perform double bypass open heart surgery on a loved one? Assuming you are not a cardiac surgeon, to preserve your ego would you say:

"I don't know shit about double bypass open heart surgery, but I can do anything I put my mind to, so hell yes I'll operate!"

OR would you say:

"Hey, I'm good at a lot of things, but I'm not good enough to perform double bypass open heart surgery on my daughter—I'm sure I'd fail."

Hopefully, the latter.

It's okay to not be good enough at something, all it means is you're not good at everything—who is? There's no shame in it. This belief reinforces your birthright to mediocrity. And best of all it's Almighty God in heaven telling you you're mediocre. And who are you to disagree with GOD? A cardiac surgeon?

Okay. Since this chapter is titled "The Five or Six Destructive Beliefs Preventing You from Achieving Happiness, Success, and Yes, Even Love," I'm going to stop here at five. You get the point and I'm getting tired. Off to bed so I don't "fail" to get my minimum twelve to fourteen hours of sleep. Goodnight.

CHAPTER 11
PINEAPPLE UPSIDE-DOWN CAKE

Qu'ils mangent de la brioche. (Let them eat brioche.*)
—Jean-Jacques Rousseau

Qu'ils mangent gâteau renversé à l'ananas. (Let them eat pineapple upside-down cake)
—M.K. Jackson

K ick it in the old school with this midcentury dessert classic. An easy-to-make and delicious-to-eat treat from a bygone era when eating baked goods, drinking hard liquor, and smoking cigarettes was good for you.

My Pineapple Upside-Down Cake Recipe

I use my big **ten-inch cast iron skillet** for baking my pineapple upside-down cake. Not only does it add midcentury authenticity, but cast iron heats evenly, making it far superior for cooking adventures.

However, if you haven't a cast iron skillet, you can use a ten-inch cake pan.

---

* Brioche is a rich bread made with eggs and butter.

Topping Ingredients:

- 1/4 cup unsalted butter
- 1/2 cup packed brown sugar
- 7 pineapple slices (canned, not fresh—it's the *midcentury way*)
- 7 maraschino cherries

Cake Ingredients:

- 1 stick (1/2 cup) unsalted butter (softened)
- 3/4 cup sugar
- 2 large eggs
- 1 teaspoon pure vanilla extract
- 1 and 1/2 cups all-purpose flour
- 1 teaspoon baking powder
- 1/4 teaspoon salt
- 5 tablespoons pineapple juice

Making the Topping

- In the cast-iron skillet, softly melt the butter over a low heat
- Mix in the brown sugar, stirring it to caramelized goodness
- Spread the butter/brown sugar mixture evenly on the bottom of the skillet (which will be the top of the cake)
- Lay the pineapple rings on top of the butter/brown sugar mixture—one in the middle, the other six around the edge Then pop the cherries into the pineapple ring holes

Batter Up!
In a bowl, the wet mixture...

- Cream the butter and sugar together
- Mix in the eggs, one at a time
- Mix in the vanilla extract

In a separate bowl, the dry mixture...

- Combine the flour, baking powder, and salt. Stir until well combined

That Takes the Cake

- With a spatula, gently fold in the dry mixture into the wet mixture (be careful not to overmix)
- Stir the pineapple juice into the batter
- Pour the cake batter into the skillet over the pineapple rings
- Place the skillet into the preheated oven
- Bake for 35 to 45 minutes (possibly more depending on the oven) until a (wood) toothpick inserted into the middle of the cake comes out clean

The Upside-Down, Rightside-Up Flip Over

- After removing the cooked cake from the oven, let it cool for about ten minutes
- Run a sharp knife around the edge of the cake to separate it from the insides of the skillet/pan
- Place a large plate/cake platter upside down on top of the skillet (which will be the bottom of the cake)
- Holding the plate to the skillet, carefully flip the two over
- Gently remove the skillet leaving the pineapple upside-down cake right side up on the plate
- Before you dig in, let the cake cool to room

temperature before slicing it (otherwise it can get rather messy)

Happiness, Success, and Yes, Even Love

Pat yourself on the back, in today's world of pre-made food at the grocery store and prepared meal delivery services, you just made a cake from what people way back in the olden days referred to as "from scratch." Chalk this up as a *success*. You'll *love* your pineapple upside-down cake. And if *it* doesn't make you *happy*, I don't what will.

CHAPTER 12

BUT ENOUGH ABOUT YOU —WHAT DO YOU THINK OF YOU?

If we cannot love ourselves, we cannot fully open to our ability to love others or our potential to create.
　—John Lennon

As a life-long Beatlemaniac, if Lennon said it, I believe it—even though he was the furthest thing from mediocre.
　—M.K. Jackson

When I was a kid growing up in the 1970s without video games, the internet, smartphones, social media, or instant 24/7 access to every movie, TV show, and song ever made, boys my age built models. Or as they were also called, "hobby kits." Whatever tickled your childhood fancy and spurred your imagination, there was a model for it: cars, motorcycles, boats and ships, military vehicles, aircraft, comic book heroes, and even torture tableaus. I liked famous cars and monsters. But my *very* favorites were spaceships (real and not). I built the Apollo LEM, the USS *Enterprise*, the Jupiter 2, and the *Millennium Falcon* among many others.

If you ask any of us Seventies kids what the best part of building models was, we won't say it was the challenge of it, or a sense of accomplishment, or even having the finished model to display. Nope. We'll all tell you the same thing: *the glue*. Testors Cement for Plastic Models—accept no substitutes. Right there, on the orange-and-white tube, in bold typeset was the reason: **DANGER FLAMMABLE VAPOR HARMFUL**. Those vapors made model building such a popular activity for us boys. It was like accidentally discovering masturbation.

I remember my first time. I was building the *Space: 1999* Eagle 1 Transporter. Slowly, the gasoline-like fumes invaded my nose, mouth, and eyes. At first, I became lightheaded. Then my brain began pulsating in color as the room wrapped around me. The induced dizziness turned into euphoria. The Eagle 1 launched into outer space with me following closely behind. Martin Landau beamed off the model kit's box and personally guided me through the galaxy.

While my friends were risking life sentences in prison trying to score half a joint from some shady character in a '74 Dodge van with smoked diamond bubble windows on the sides, I bought this glorious tube of hallucinogenic ecstasy from a clerk at a *toy store*. Yes, that is correct, *in 1974 a ten-year-old child could purchase a Schedule 1 controlled substance over the counter in a fucking toy store*. Dude, the 70s—fuck yeah!

Granted, I didn't huff the shit with the collective power of the Ramones as some of my friends did, but nor did I proactively deter the fumes from innocently wafting into my nasal passages and providing an "accidental" high I so fondly long for to this day.

When building models, I'd first cut all the pieces from the sprues using a sharp knife (safety first!) and lay them out on the table, arranged as shown in the instructions, all ready for assembly. The diagram of zig-zagging dashed lines led by arrows mapped the pathway to a perfectly assembled Ironside Van (complete with power ramp and Ironside's wheelchair) from the hit NBC crime show starring Raymond Burr.*

---

* Apparently, when the fine folks at the MPC hobby kit corporation (part of the

But all that painstaking prep work of cutting the parts, filing the rough edges, reading the instructions, and selecting just the right color paints was all for naught if I didn't have the glue. Without the glue, all I had was a pile of plastic and rubber bits and pieces. Without the glue, I couldn't cement the parts together into a fully realized model ready for display. And without the glue, I didn't get that exhilarating high.

Building Your Model Life

Think of this book as the instructions to building your model life of happiness, success, and yes, even love. When assembling the chapters you'll need to provide the glue that holds it all together. However, this glue is not something you'll have to buy from a pseudo-pharmaceutical toy dealer. It's an *ability* you already have within you. And if you read the quote at the top of the chapter you already know what it is...

Self-love.

Self-love is the glue that cements together everything in this book. It's the most significant component in building the new you. It's safe to use, comes with no warnings, no danger, and no flammable vapors—but it still provides that euphoric high. No question about it, self-love is integral to a life of happiness, success, and love. More than journaling. More than affirmations. And especially more than getting up five hours earlier in the morning.

Before I discuss exactly what self-love is, I want to take a moment and address what it *isn't*. Loving yourself does not mean you become a narcissist. Narcissistic personality disorder

---

"Fun Group" at General Mills) were looking for a beloved 1970s action TV series character for a model kit that would excite ten-year-old boys, rather than choosing the Six Million Dollar Man, Starsky and/or Hutch, or any of Charlie's Angels (the obvious choice), their research naturally led them to a middle-aged, wheelchair using, cop with paraplegia brought to life by that icon of 70s youth culture, Raymond Burr. Nailed it!

is a mental condition in which people have an inflated sense of their own importance, a deep need for excessive attention and admiration, engage in troubled relationships, and display a lack of empathy for others.[1] Don't be a narcissist.

Neither is self-love the same as self-*confidence*. Self-confidence is trust in your abilities, capacities, and judgment.[2] Self-love, on the other hand, is the belief that you are a *valuable* and *worthy* person.[3] Ironically, you can be self-confident without self-love, as in being confident that you are not valuable or worthy—which is why it's critical not to interchange the two.

When we think of loving someone to make our lives richer and more complete we rarely think of *ourselves* as that person. But you will never receive the happiness, success, and love you want—and *deserve*—in your life until you truly know and deeply *believe*, in your heart and soul that you are worthy of it in all its forms, variations, and purchases.

With self-love, you embrace and accept not only who you are, but what you are capable (and incapable) of—not punishing yourself for everything you are not that others are. Whether you run a multibillion-dollar company or make minimum wage at a fast-food restaurant, you are deserving. This is one area where career success definitely does NOT make one single bit of difference.

Finally, and perhaps most essential, self-love brings authenticity to your life. Everything you say and do, the actions you take, and the decisions you make are genuinely supportive of your best interests—as opposed to *staging* yourself to impress potential buyers. By loving and respecting yourself, you won't accept only what you can get, and you'll never settle for less than you deserve.

When we operate from self-love we are more forgiving of ourselves. Our confidence increases. Our perspective widens. We become more resilient, making it easier to bounce back from adversity because we believe ourselves to be able and unshakable, and most of all, *deserving* of it. Our path to happiness, success, and love is shorter, more direct, and far more easily attained. It's virtually *automatic*!

Worthy? Valued? Deserving? But I Thought I Was Mediocre

You are. I am too. So are 98+ percent of the world's population. However, there's a difference between mediocrity's capability to *achieve* and self-love's capacity to *receive*. It's that combination of the two that creates happiness, success, and love without trying too hard.

At first glance, mediocrity and self-love may seem strange bedfellows. *No self-loving person would allow themselves to be mediocre!* On the contrary, *only* a self-loving person can allow themselves to be mediocre because only a self-loving person accepts themselves as who they really are—mediocrity and all.

The Road to Self-Love Does Not Include a Detour Through Self-Criticism

Some folks believe being self-critical is necessary for self-improvement and, subsequently, self-growth. Nothing could be further from the truth. Being self-critical has a far closer relation to self-sabotage than it does self-improvement. Why? Because **you are *not* qualified to criticize yourself**. Don't believe me? Well then let me put it this way: **you are *not* qualified to criticize yourself**. And if that is not clear enough then maybe this is: **you are *not* qualified to criticize yourself**.

Now, you're probably thinking *I'm the only one qualified to criticize myself because I know myself better than anyone else does.* No, you aren't and no, you don't. I know this with irrevocable authority because when it comes to self-criticism, I am *the best* at it—it's something I could write a book about. I played my Self-Criticism World Tour to sold-out shows and rave reviews: "You're so hard on yourself!" "You wouldn't talk that way about your worst enemy!!" "You need to ease up on yourself!!!" All to which I would reply: *I'm not being self-critical. It's simply reporting the facts.* But I've come to learn (if not always able to accept) that even *if* my "brutally honest" assessment of my life were true, the question remains: *what good does it do me?* Does it make me more successful? Is it cause for happiness in my life? Is it a surefire turn-on for potential romantic partners? (The answers, by the way, in order of asking are: "no," "no," and "no.")

The Shortcut to Not Trying So Hard

Through self-love, the sources of happiness, success, and love are *within* you—which really cuts down on all the R&D time. This is nothing new. We've all heard the cliché *true happiness comes from within.* We've also heard the cliché *you cannot love someone else until you love yourself.* And we all know a cliché is a cliché because it's true. Therefore, I am now adding my own cliché into the mix: *You don't pull happiness, success, and love outta your ass, you pull it outta yourself.*

So how then can I help you express self-love quickly and without excessive and/or unnecessary endeavor? Well, thanks to my moist, mildewy walls, I have the answer.

I recently bought a dehumidifier for my home. This thing's amazing. It magically sucks moisture out of the air and turns it into water—that I use for my plants, toilet, making coffee, whatever. Point of this story is I'm not Luke Skywalker, I don't know fuck all about moisture farming. And since I don't have a droid that understands the binary language of moisture vaporators (or speaks Bocce), I used the *quick start guide* to get the gizmo up and running.

One morning, while working on this chapter, tired of thinking and sick of typing, I struggled for a quick and EZ way to present the benefits of self-love. As I took another sip of my freshly brewed condensation coffee, it suddenly dawned on me: *this fucking coffee is made with room sweat! Why the fuck am I drinking this air piss??? It's fulla dust mites and swamp ass, ass farts and fly shit 'cause, like birds, flies just shit in the air when they're flying around. I drank like fifteen cups of this liquid smegma. Sonuvabitch! Now that crap's gonna be in my intestines, bladder, and my urethra. My fucking urethra, goddamnit!*

I was violently sick to my stomach. I remembered my Cub Scout training (or was it Webelos?) to induce vomiting. I threw up all over my kitchen floor. The sight and smell of the vomit made me even sicker. I vomited again. Now, I was nauseous *and* light-headed. The room spun around me, my legs buckled, and I fell to the floor, my landing softened by the pool of puke.

I assessed my situation: flat on my back, sick, dizzy, my ass soaked in vomitus eruptus.

This is when I do my best work.

Okay, I began thinking. *Back to where I was before this sidetrack into botulistic writer's block... express self-love... quick and EZ... moist, mildewy walls... dehumidifier... Luke Skywalker... quick start guide...* BOOM!

And that, dear readers, is a peek behind the curtain at my writing process in action. The result of which is...

The Non-mildew, No-Fly-Shit Quick Start Guide to Self-Love for Happiness, Success, and Love without Liquid Smegma (Coffee Optional)

It's everything you need to know about self-love's contributions to your happiness, success, and love in expurgated, bite-sized chunks. Beginning with...

Happiness

When you love someone you make them happy. So, why not try it on yourself? Here's how self-love contributes to *your* happiness...

- **you're empowered with belief in yourself**—and no one can take that away from you;
- **you're no longer concerned with other people's opinions of you**—Here's a delicious nugget of wisdom dipped in sweet & spicy insight sauce that has served me well: *What other people think of me is none of my business;*
- **from self-love comes a healthier you**—and a healthy life is a happy life;
- **you love yourself enough to follow your own heart**—and that's always a great place to end up;
- **you'll take care of your own needs before taking care of others**—put your oxygen mask on first, before assisting others.

Success
Self-love contributes to your success by providing you with…

- **increased confidence**—when you believe in yourself, there's no stopping you;
- **the ability to handle adversity**—so you'll bounce right back;
- **clearer perspective**—for better decision-making;
- **fearlessness (AKA Courage) to take risks**—without risk, there is no reward;
- **sharper intuition**—no more second-guessing and doubting yourself.

Love
Your intimate relationships blossom and thrive when you first love yourself. Here's why…

- **you no longer need validation from others**—it's exhausting for your partner to love you enough for the both of you;

- **you'll no longer tolerate those who don't respect and value you**—we teach people how to treat us;
- **you can kiss codependency goodbye**—it's nice not to be needy;
- **you have confidence**—ain't nothing sexier than having someone who's comfortable in their own skin—and yours;
- **you know when it's time to walk away and you can do it**—I realize this seems like a bummer, but no one does anyone any favors stealing years from each other's lives by staying in a bad relationship—romantic or platonic.

Love to Love You, Baby

I know, I know... You thought you were reading a book on making it with mediocrity then all of a sudden WHAM! out of left field, I hit you with this self-love stuff. I realize it comes across as touchy-feely. And I also understand how it may seem contradictory to the whole mediocrity principle. Put another log in the fire... The only way I can explain that is to tell you a story, about myself...

At first, it wasn't easy accepting that I was part of the mediocre majority. I struggled with the *guilt* it caused because I, like so many others, was programmed to believe that I must always do better, be better, and am better. And once I did make the commitment to mediocrity, I then felt *shame. Guilt + shame* = self-loathing. *And self-loathing* is such an uncompassionate way to think of yourself, wouldn't you agree?

So, I asked myself, *what's the opposite of such a brutal view of myself?* The answer was obvious: *self-love.* Embracing self-love removed that guilt and shame and replaced it with *acceptance.*

For much of my life, I predicated my happiness on the approval of others: parents, family, friends, schoolmates, coworkers, women, even strangers. Then I realized there's one person missing from that list: *me*. So, I decided to cut out the middleman and pass the savings directly on to me. I put more personal importance on *me* accepting me than I did on other people doing so, and I did it with self-love.

By now, you're hopefully thinking to yourself: *Okay, I'm sold on this self-love thing, it sounds pretty fantastic! So tell me: how can I get me some?* The good news is there are several simple methods available to cultivate your very own supply of self-love. And fortunately, I have a leftover chapter where I can write them down for you...

CHAPTER 13

A HOW-TO GUIDE TO SELF-LOVE

If you have the ability to love, love yourself first.
— Charles Bukowski

If you have the ability to read, read Bukowski first.
—M.K. Jackson

While the benefits of self-love(ing) are immeasurable, self-love is, unfortunately, something that does not come easy to many of us.

Here are twenty things you can do for your *body, mind,* and *spirit* to help get yourself in the mood for (self-)love.

Body

Your body is a temple (mine's more like a convenience store).

1. Eat healthy. Nourishing foods that make your body thrive. I'm not a nutritionist so I can't get too specific, but usually, something off a tree or from the ground can be good.

2. Stay hydrated. Every cell in your body needs proper hydration to function properly. That's why I drink ten to twelve cups of coffee each day (with electrolytes, of course). But I hear water works too.

3. Exercise. It gives you energy, relieves stress, and keeps you mentally alert. Exercise can also help depression, your heart, and sleeping. The Mayo Clinic recommends at least 30 minutes of moderate physical activity every day. This includes activities such as brisk walking, biking, swimming, and mowing the lawn.[1]

4. Get plenty of sleep. Personally, I'm no good without my regular twelve to fourteen hours a day. However, for most legal adults, sleep experts recommend seven to nine hours a day. Restful, restorative sleep promotes emotional stability, focused concentration, improved digestion, and a stronger immune system. When you're sleeping, the brain can repair and grow cells, tissue, and nerves that regenerate and boost the hormone and immune system.[2]

I LOVE these facts because, if nothing else, they prove those so-called "self-improvement gurus" making you lose sleep so you can get up five hours earlier each day to journal are out of their minds. *Be happy and successful—stay in bed, stay asleep.*

5. Hygiene: keep it clean. Keeping your body clean is an expression of self-love because it's self-*care*. We keep the things we most care about clean and maintained. We wash our car, clean our house, and launder our clothes. Our bodies are no different. And I'm not only talking about the dirt and grime that piles up on our bodies over the course of a normal day, there's also the internally produced and secreted detritus. The human body is a gross waste factory that constantly manufactures sweat, oil, mucus, snot, dead cells, dandruff, and head cheese. Fun fact: we shed around 600,000 dead skin cells per day, up to 1.5 pounds of skin cells per year.[3] Yikes!

You don't want all that crap in and on your body, turning you into a walking toxic dump. Remember the three Ss of good hygiene: *Shit, Shower,* and *Shave* (that last one only pertains to those who identify as hirsute). To that list I would add BSG: *brush* your teeth, *shampoo* your hair, and *groom* your ass.

A good rule of thumb for self-loving personal hygiene is your body should be cleaner than your car—*inside and outside*. (If you don't have a car then the rule of thumb is your body should be cleaner than your oven—*inside and out*.)

6. Floss. This is something that seems to pop up on every "good things for you to do" list so what the hell?—I'm including it here, too. I mean, it can't hurt—they *are* your choppers after all. You don't get another set, so take care of them.

Mind

7. Forgive yourself. We can be our own worst enemies. We can hold grudges for our past mistakes and mercilessly criticize our failings. But there is nothing you have done (or haven't done) to you that's worth punishing yourself for. We often forgive the ones we love for their transgression, you deserve the same from yourself. You're human, you make mistakes—and you're sure to make more. Accept your humanness. Life is so much easier with a daily clean slate.

8. Start each day on a positive note. When you wake up, the first thing out of your mouth should be something nice to yourself (*Good morning, [your name here]...Today's a new day with new possibilities... I'm going to have a great day today whether I like it or not... Boy, your hair looks great first thing in the morning* [but only if it actually does]).

The first action you take (after urinating, of course) should be something nurturing for yourself (meditate/pray, breakfast, coffee, sex).

The first thing you do in the morning should NEVER be to check your phone/computer/tablet. Yeah, I know what you're doing—you're checking social media, you're getting the news, and you're poisoning your new day before it even begins. Don't worry, all the exciting, earth-shattering events on social media and negative, horrid events on the news will still be there after you get yourself off to a great start for the day. And who knows?

Maybe by then, you'll be feeling so good, you won't need that detrimental data dump.

Oh, and if you cannot think of something positive to start your day, see number six.

9. Set boundaries. With everything and everyone. When you set boundaries, you lay down the law on how others should treat you. Healthy boundaries ensure *your* needs are met. They show that you respect yourself and demand the same from others. When we let other people take advantage of us, we often become angry and resentful of them. Setting boundaries is a surefire way to improve all your relationships. Tip: a test to measure how much a boundary is needed is how strongly people react to it. The harder they push back, the more necessary the boundary.

10. Just say "no." Sure, it didn't work for dope, but it *will* work for you. It's hard to tell people "no." Believe me, I'm afflicted with the *disease to please*. But a lot of times what people ask of you isn't for your own good, it's for theirs. Ask yourself: do I really want to do this? Telling someone "no" doesn't make you a bad person, it makes you a strong person. It's not being rude, it's honoring *you*. Oh, and when you say "no," you needn't give elaborate reasons why. Like they say: *No is a complete sentence*.

11. End toxic relationships. You don't leave spoiled food in your refrigerator. It takes up space, it smells, and it has no nutritional value. In fact, it can make you sick. Think of toxic people as taking up space in your fridge, adding no nutritional value to your life, while making you sick to your stomach (some of them may even smell). Interpersonal relationships should nourish and delight. There's only so much space in your life; don't fill it with rancid people. Choose friends who respect and honor you while giving you the opportunity to do the same for them. If not, it's time to throw out those rotten eggs.

12. Stop requiring approval from others. C'mon, say it with me: *what other people think of me is none of my business*. You're reading this book, examining your rules, values, and beliefs, figuring out ways to twist life's circumstances in your favor, and doing it all while passionately embracing your mediocrity. After all that, why would you let some jackass, who hasn't done the same, influence your opinion of yourself?

13. Stop comparing yourself—to other people and other things. It doesn't matter that you don't make as much money as your enemies do. Or that your best friend's spouse is better looking than yours. Or that you had to settle for a townhouse even though all your friends and brothers have a regular house with a backyard or a garage like you had when you were a kid. *None* of these comparisons matter (well, some less than others. That better-looking spouse one can be pretty rough, especially in social occasions). When you love and accept yourself for who you are, comparing is not only ridiculous, it's offensive—to *you*.

I'm not suggesting that we cannot pursue things and people we want (like your best friend's spouse)—just not as a yardstick to measure our failure (or success). Personally, I've never joyfully pursued anything motivated by envy—and if I did manage to get it, I was never really gratified by it (well, maybe by my *enemy's* spouse).

Spirit

14. Calm your mind every day. Whether it's meditating, praying, breathing, or just sitting quietly for a while, clearing your mind of thoughts and *being in the moment* does wonders for your mental and psychological clarity (even your physical energy as well). It helps you cut through all the white noise so you can focus on what really matters in your life.

15. Express gratitude every day. *Psychology Today* claims there are scientifically proven benefits from expressing gratitude in our lives including improved physical and psychological health, enhanced empathy, reduced aggression, and increased self-esteem.[4] But the three *best* things about expressing gratitude are:

- it's EZ—takes very little effort;
- it's FREE—doesn't cost anything;
- it can be simple—what you're grateful for needn't be big-ass fancy-pants stuff. It can be the most modest of things that you were freely given: family, friends, memories, a blue sky, another day of life.

Many people even make gratitude *lists* every single day so th—

STOP!

I am in *no way* suggesting you go overboard on this gratitude thing by writing shit down every *day* because:

- it's dangerously close to journaling;
- it's a lot of work.

However, I can offer you a clever workaround that I use as a safeguard to prevent overdoing it when I'm forced to write things down. I purchase these little notepads from the Amazon.com. They're a minuscule 2-1/4 inches by 3-1/2 inches with only twenty tiny pages and just nine lines on each page—that means a whole lotta less writing. Plus, I write BIG so I can't fit any more than like, six words per page, that way there's no danger of turning my quick notes into journaling. Get some for yourself and be *grateful* you don't have to write a lot.

16. Live with purpose. What is the meaning of life? Monty Python figured it out: *Try and be nice to people, avoid eating fat, read a good book every now and then, get some walking in, and try and live together in peace and harmony with people of all creeds and nations.*

But you're not Monty Python so you're stuck with having to figure out the meaning of your own life. Like a good story, life is so much more satisfying when it has a point. What's the purpose (or purpoi) of your life? Again, you're not looking for some monumental accomplishment for humanity here (there are already *plenty* of those from people far greater than the rest of us). You're not doing anyone any favors (first and foremost yourself) by betraying your own mediocrity in favor of some foolhardy ideal so grandiose in its design that it fosters the endless pursuit of an unachievable aspiration—*that* is insanity.

Your purpose can be something as simple (read: EZ) as mediocre family, mediocre friends, mediocre career, mediocre creativity, mediocre spiritual harmony, mediocre service, or just mediocrity itself. Whatever it is, when you live your life's purpose, then all you say and do supports it. That's when you'll start succeeding more in life and feeling better about yourself in the process—a mediocre process.

17. Love and respect others. I know what you're thinking: *Hey, this is supposed to be about loving me! Why do I have to love and respect others?* One word: *The Golden Rule*. We feel so much better about ourselves when we're treating others in the way we want to be treated.

18. Be creative. Creativity is the divine spark within all of us. Expressing your creativity is as much a spiritual practice as it is a pleasurable activity. Thanks to your day job, you're already doing all the spreadsheeting, programming, organizing, analyzing, managing, stocking, contracting, constructing, cracking, crunching, tabulating, reporting, shipping, clocking inning, clocking outing, and commuting that a human being should have to do. Give the left side of your brain a welcome break and let the right side do the driving for a while. Painting, sculpting, writing, photography, music, cooking, gardening, origami, making stuff, and building models with model glue are all ways of expressing your creativity.

WARNING! When being creative, you are *not* allowed to be your own worst creative critic. Sure, you're not Picasso, Leonardo, Maya Angelou, Jean-Luc Godard, Jane Austen, Katsushika Oi, John Coltrane, Frida Kahlo, or The Beatles—who is? Recall number twelve on this list, and don't compare yourself to other folks—*especially* folks like those I just mentioned who are super-human mutants at the highest level of excellence in their chosen field. They're part of that one-to-two percent of humanity who doesn't need to read this book. Mediocrity is not their guiding force. So, while it's okay that they *inspire* you, don't let them *retire* you—this is *not* a contest. Art (or at least *your* art) is subjective and, therefore, critic-proof.

19. Go easy on yourself. How many times have you heard this? *You are your own worst enemy.* As I stated earlier, **you are *not* qualified to criticize yourself.** You're too close to the subject. Besides, with self-love and mediocrity in your corner, you don't have to work so hard analyzing your past errors in order to make calculated improvements.

Being hard on yourself is completely unhealthy and unproductive. It's all about the value you add to your life and the lives of others—and there is no value in crucifying yourself (Believe me, I know this, I was raised Catholic).

20. Give yourself a reach around and pat yourself on the back. Next time you accomplish something, reach around and give yourself a pat on ass, no matter how big or small (the accomplishment, not your ass)—getting a superlative annual review at work, getting a so-so annual review at work, getting a shitty annual review at work, going grocery shopping, paying your rent/mortgage, making it to another anniversary, making it to another birthday, making it to another day, finishing reading a book on achieving happiness, success, and love through the unbridled power of mediocrity, finishing writing a book on happiness, success, and love through the unbridled power of mediocrity, or even just getting up in the morning (aim for the middle, don't be a hero).

Whatever it is, do something special for yourself... dinner, a movie, mini golf, sex (with someone else *or* yourself), visit a museum, the beach, or the circus, buy yourself a Ouija board, stay overnight at a cheap roadside motel (with or without the sex and/or the Ouija).

21. Have some fun! Get off your ass and do something that tickles your fancy (which can include tickling your fancy ass).

Once you finish this book, you will no longer need to expend so much time and effort achieving happiness, success, and love so you'll have plenty of time left over to do something FUN! Take dancing lessons, take a cooking class, take public transportation, throw a Tupperware party, attend a séance (with your new Ouija board), or create a fun, new email address for yourself like *Dick_Hertz_69@hotmail.com* (don't waste your time, I already own it).

Pursuing a You-nogamous Relationship

Self-love actually requires far less time and effort than a relationship with another. Yet, cultivating, nurturing, and practicing a loving relationship with oneself can be a heavier lift because so many of us feel unworthy of our own love (let alone someone else's).

If you're unable to fully embrace and love yourself, I highly encourage you to really get to know you in a different, more intimate way. There are oodles of excellent videos, podcasts, books, courses, and webinars by the top self-lovers in their field that can help you woo yourself.

So, why all this effort to win yourself over when there're plenty of other fish to see? Because, self-love is the intoxicating vapor glue that cements you to your happiness, success, and love.

Still skeptical? We haven't put all the parts together yet...

PART TWO
PUTTING IT ALL TOGETHER

CHAPTER 14
YOUR HAPPY, SUCCESSFUL, LOVING LIFE (PART 2)

To succeed in life, you need two things: ignorance and confidence.
—Mark Twain

A life of realized adequacy is far more fulfilling than one of elusive excellence.
—M. K. Jackson

B elieve it or not, most folks never take the time to actually define, with clarity and precision, what happiness, success, and love are for them. If you count yourself among this group, don't fret, we're going to remedy that now using my unique proprietary technology, patent not pending, EZ-2-do, **four-step process to authentic happiness, success, and yes, even love**.

If you are someone who has defined your own happiness, success, and love I encourage you to still forge ahead with these four steps and reexamine the definitions you have—the results may surprise you.

Now, I realize the mere mention of the word "results" can cause anxiety, worry, tension, and fear because "results" are predicated upon instigating action, exerting effort, and following through to produce said "results"—all of which require *work*. Regretfully, that is true in this case—but to a much lesser degree than other self-realization books, programs, webinars, and masterminds.

With my system, the work and effort are all *front-loaded*. It's not like keeping in great physical shape where you must keep exercising to maintain results. Nope. Once you finish these four steps, that's it, you're done. No more work required. Yay! Best self-realization program *ever*!

DEAR Happiness, Success, and Love...

Define, Evaluate, Align, Redefine.

I call my process DEAR because the word is a term of endearment, a form of address expressing deep affection, and it's also used as an exclamation as in *Oh, dear!* The process you are about to undertake is an exclamation of affection toward yourself through the self-loving gifts of happiness, success, and love in your life. So, I've given it the name DEAR.

Okay...I admit it. That's all bullshit.

The acronym "DEAR" really makes no sense whatsoever within the context of redesigning happiness, success, and love using newly defined rules, values, and beliefs through the application of mediocrity. Truth is it just happened that the words I used for each step by chance spelled "DEAR." Sure, I would've loved an acronym like ACT, but that's not enough steps (and it sounds like a college entrance exam), or ACTION, but that's too many steps (and sounds like an over-the-counter laxative). So, I'm stuck with DEAR. But please don't let the lame name fool you, it's still a highly effective and proven process. C'mon, I'll show you...

Step 1: *Define* Your Happiness, Success, and Love

We start off low and slow as it is the way to go. The first step is the easiest part of the process for people (and when I say "people" I mean *me* since this book is the first time I've run this by someone other than myself). You'll write down what you (currently) think it takes for you to feel happy, successful, and in love. No filtering. No editing. No judgment. No applying what you've read thus far. Just whatever you need for happiness, success, and love.

Step 2: *Evaluate* Your Definitions of Happiness, Success, and Love

The diagnostic step. Applying the knowledge freshly gained from this book (see? I told you you had to read the whole thing), you'll assess your definitions and suss out these three annihilators of happiness, success, and love:

- *contradictions*
- *improbabilities*
- *impossibilities*

During the process, you'll likely discover that what's been preventing you from being genuinely happy, successful, and truly in love is the very list you composed.

Step 3: *Align* Your Rules, Values, and Beliefs

Having exposed your definitions of happiness, success, and love for the frauds they are, you'll now focus your critical eye on what made them so foolhardy in the first place: your rules, values, and beliefs.

All three are the filters through which you formulate virtually every decision you make. But because they were primarily installed in you by other people, institutions, and organizations to benefit their agendas, they often represent disparate ways of seeing the world and, even worse, are usually in conflict with one another. In step 3, you'll take ownership of your happiness, success, and love by aligning your rules, values, and beliefs with *your* agenda.

Step 4: *Redefine* Your Definitions of Happiness, Success, and Love

It's time to grab destiny by the nads and squeeze out new, *realizable* definitions of happiness, success, and love—and in step 4, you're gonna squeeze hard.

This is where the technologies, techniques, tactics, and tools I've presented in this book, including not trying so hard, driving your own car, rules/values/beliefs, lemons into whisky sours, and, of course, the power of mediocrity, all coalesce into the new blueprint for your happy, successful, loving life. Plus, there is one last secret ingredient we'll add to make your new definitions more real, authentic, and fulfilling than the previous ones... Agog? I'll give you a hint: *it begins with "e" and ends with "motion."*

Prepare for DEAR —*man, that's such a lame acronym*

There's no way of pussy footing around it. Each of the four steps you are about to undertake will require *some* effort on your part. Each contains written lessercises that you'll have to put *some* thought into.

Due to the "workshop" nature of the four steps, you should tackle the four steps rested and hydrated (but not too hydrated; frequent bathroom breaks can disrupt the creative momentum). And while I normally consider cocktails a form of hydration, in this case, it's probably best to participate in the workshop sober.

That should do it. Once you have that piece of paper and writing utensil, meet me back here.

Oh boy, are we gonna have some fun!

CHAPTER 15
STEP 1: DEFINE YOUR HAPPINESS, SUCCESS, AND LOVE

Strong people define themselves; weak people allow others to define them.

—Ken Poirot

I don't have a problem with others defining me—so long as they are correct in their definition.

—M.K. Jackson

Step 1 in putting it all together is to *define* your current criteria of happiness, success, and love.

Remember back in chapter 2 when I instructed you to write down your definitions of success, happiness, and love and then throw them away? In retrospect I wish I hadn't done that (told you to chuck them) because they'd come in handy right now. It's just that it made for such a great dramatic ending to the chapter.

Damn.

Unless... depending on how fast you read this book... you might remember back to what you wrote, or at least the highlights. Or maybe the paper's still in your trash and you can retrieve it. That would be great. Hopefully, it's not soaked in Fettuccine Alfredo or pudding and it's still legible.

Then again, you may have emptied the garbage. Crap. In that

case, I guess you could go out and root around in the trash bin for it. But if your garbage has been hauled away, then the pieces of that list are long gone, on their way to a floating barge somewhere in the middle of the Atlantic Ocean to be picked over by seagulls (who ironically can't even eat fettuccini or pudding because they don't have lips).

If that's the case, then that list is gone for good, and you'll just have to redo it. Sorry about that, I know how much I hate having to do redundant work. But it shouldn't be too difficult since you've been living with these definitions for a while now.

Whether you remember your definitions or they're floating out to sea where exasperated, lipless gulls futilely attempt to suck the caked Fettuccine Alfredo and pudding from them, let's get cracking on step 1...

WARNING! EFFORT ALERT!
The following section involves thinking and writing. A modicum of time and effort on the part of you, the reader, will be required.

To ensure maximum benefit with minimal effort, please remember to follow these three rules:

1. Use a *single* piece of paper for the lessercise—more pages = more work.
2. Do *not* use a computer for the lessercises—embrace the *Three Ps*: paper, pencil, pen.
3. Do *not* overthink the lessercises—overthinking is overrated.

Introducing the *Graphical Representation of Improved Definitions* (GRID)

On your paper, using your darkest-colored writing utensil,

draw **three columns and four rows**. In the top row, above columns two and three—wait…

Before continuing, I just have to take a second to express my complete happiness and total satisfaction with this GRID acronym. It's everything that dumb-ass DEAR one isn't: strong, descriptive, and to the point. And best of all, it's absolutely apposite. I mean, it's a *graphic*, it's a *representation*, the *definitions* are going to be *improved*, and it's all in a grid that's called GRID! Outstanding. Everything I've ever wanted in my dream acronym!

Okay, so back to the grid… As I said, in the top row, above columns two and three, write *NOW* and *NEW*. Then, under the first column, in rows two, three, and four, write *HAPPINESS*, *SUCCESS*, and *LOVE*. You should have a GRID that looks like this (figure 15.1):

Figure 15.1

Next, in the *NOW* column, in the *HAPPINESS*, *SUCCESS*, and *LOVE* rows, **write three ways/things that define each of**

them for yourself (before you began reading this book). When finished, you should have nine things total—three for happiness, three for success, and three for love.

I've included my personal grid as an example, complete with my own **original** definitions* (figure 15.2).

Figure 15.2

At the time, I believed these definitions accurately represented everything I needed to be happy, successful, and loving. They were the guiding force in my life—and that was the problem. But we'll address that in the next step. For now, just get all your definitions into the grid.

For those of you who cannot read my handwriting (or purchased the discount version of the book sans illustrations), let's review my previous definitions...

---

* While you can copy my grid for yours, it's imperative you use your own definitions of success, happiness, and love. DO NOT copy my definitions as your own. I appreciate you embracing the whole "not trying too hard" thing, but that's taking it a bit too far.

Happiness

1. *A pet giraffe*
2. *Revenge on my enemies*
3. *Being of service*

Success

1. *Be a rich and famous author*
2. *Sex with a supermodel*
3. *Make people do my bidding*

Love

1. *Marriage*
2. *My own family*
3. *Adoration of others*

Now it's your turn. Fill in your grid with your three definitions each of success, happiness, and love as they pertain to *your* life. Remember: don't overthink it. Go with what you already have (that's the point of this step). Don't spend too much time on it. And most of all, don't try too hard.

I'll be waiting right here when you're finished.

.

.

.

Welcome back. Give yourself a well-deserved pat on the back. You have completed the all-important first step. And you know that old saying, *the most happy, successful, loving journey begins with step 1.*

I'd love to hear your definitions, but this being a book, that's pretty much not gonna happen. However, I'm betting there's lots of room for plenty of evaluation (as there was with my definitions)—and that's a good thing. A *very* good thing. The more evaluation you do, the better you can whip those suckers into shape for guaranteed, unconditional, and effortless happiness, success, and love in your life.

If you need a break, feel free to take one—but not too long, we're on a roll!

When you're ready to continue, grab your completed definitions GRID and meet me in step 2.

CHAPTER 16
STEP 2: EVALUATE YOUR DEFINITIONS OF HAPPINESS, SUCCESS, AND LOVE

When I let go of what I am, I become what I might be.
—Lao Tzu

When I let go, I fall on my ass.
—M.K. Jackson

Step 2 in putting it all together is to *evaluate* your definitions. Rarely do we take time to define what would truly make us *feel* happy, successful, and loving. All too often we carelessly allow others to define our success, happiness, and love for us. And when we do, we're usually given *defective definitions*—a random collection of outdated, one-size-fits-all dogmatic assumptions dooming us to failure, misery, and loneliness.

Fortunately, defective definitions can be corrected and restored to perfect working condition. But first, as with all trouble shooting, the problem must be identified and isolated.

WARNING! EFFORT ALERT!
The following section involves thinking and writing. A modicum of time and effort on the part of you, the reader, will be required.

For maximum benefit with minimal effort, please remember to follow these three rules:

1. Use *the same GRID* you already made and used in step 1 for the lessercise—more pages = more work.
2. Do *not* use a computer for the lessercises—embrace the *Three Ps*: paper, pencil, pen.
3. Do *not* overthink the lessercises—overthinking is overrated.

Don't let that warning scare you. As promised, step 2 is a quick and EZ process. You're going to analyze each of your three definitions of happiness, success, and love, looking for one or more of these malignancies:

1. *Conflicts*—The definition opposes and/or contradicts one or both of your other definitions. This conflict cancels out one or more of the definitions, making it impossible for them to be successfully realized.
2. *Improbabilities*—The definition is unlikely to happen. Not that it cannot happen, just that it probably won't. Some reasons for the improbability include (but are not limited to): *reality* and *trying too hard*.
3. *Impossibilities*—The definition is so pie in the sky that no [minimal] amount of time or mediocre effort could *ever* manifest this definition.

The very presence of any one or more of these virulent qualities within a category or even *across* categories firmly inserts a wedge between you and your happiness, success, and love.

To assist you in evaluating your definitions, I'm going to walk you through the process I used to identify the *conflicts*, *improbabilities*, and *impossibilities* in my original set of definitions for happiness, success, and love...

. . .

Happiness

1. *A pet giraffe*
2. *Revenge on my enemies*
3. *Being of service*

Number one, **a pet giraffe**. Ever since I visited Uganda and saw giraffes up close, I've been fascinated by, and enamored of them. They are so unique compared to other animals...

- Giraffes are the tallest animals on earth.
- No two giraffes have the same spots.
- Giraffes sleep only 30 minutes in total each day.
- Their long-ass necks have only seven vertebrae, just like the human neck.
- Their long-ass necks can't reach the ground.
- A group of giraffes is known as a *tower*.
- They can run as fast as thirty-seven miles an hour.
- They hum to communicate with each other (tending to hum at night).
- Giraffes can go without water for up to three days.
- The average life span of a giraffe is twenty-five years.

Those facts, plus that I *love* animals, made having a pet giraffe a no-brainer—as in no brain was used in making that decision.

First, my townhouse's HOA has a thirty-five-pound maximum weight for pets. Second, I have a tiny patio and there's no way a giraffe can get up to thirty miles an hour in that space even if it ran in a circle.

But all that's irrelevant because I live in the city of Los Angeles, not the Savannah of Uganda so I don't know what the fuck you feed a giraffe in captivity. Even with its long-ass neck, there's not enough vegetation available and I have no clue what to feed a goddamned giraffe. Purina Giraffe Chow? And where the hell do I even get giraffe food? *Not* at PetCo or Trader Joe's. I checked. I guess I could get some from the zoo but they only sell animal food in those tiny ice cream cones. I'd go broke and have a ton of Scoopy's cake cups left over.

Of course, I could just go to where everyone else goes for hard-to-find items: the dark web. But since I don't even know what giraffe food looks like I'd probably get ripped off by some unscrupulous animal food counterfeiter. Hell, I don't even know how to get on the dark web. Is there an app for that?

But all the worry over giraffe food isn't the real problem because if the giraffe eats, it follows the giraffe shits. And given the size of a giraffe, I'm guessing it's gonna be a shit ton of crap. And one thing I do know about happiness, it is definitely *not* shoveling giraffe shit every day. So, color this one a resounding, flag-waving, card-carrying *impossibility*.

Definitions number two, *revenge on my enemies*, and number three, *being of service,* are both, in and of themselves, fantastic answers. Gobs of social organizations, religious institutions, and self-care programs promote being of service as a means to achieving true happiness. And the pure joy of raining down biblical-grade high-octane hell-fire vengeance upon the heads of those who have wronged me cannot be dismissed—just ask politicians, scorned spouses, and Klingons.

Unfortunately, the two *conflict* with each other. Both are sure to make me happy—*but not at the same time*. I cannot be of service to humanity if I'm simultaneously serving up ice-cold dishes of revenge against it. Thus, I have painted myself into a failure corner and can rule out any hopes of happiness in my future.

Success

1. *A rich and famous author*
2. *Sex with a supermodel*
3. *Make people do my bidding*

Okay, right off the bat, definition number one, **a rich and famous author**, squarely falls into the category of **improbability** with two specific problems: the *rich* and the *famous* parts. There's too much packed into it. Rich *and* famous and an *author*? Jesus, why not add "who owns the fucking moon" in there too? Authors are not rock stars. Wealth and fame are not part and parcel of the occupation of littérateur. (Remember, *specificity is the silent killer of dreams.*)

Rich. How? By writing books that no one reads because they're from an author nobody knows? Given the current sales paradigm for books, I have a better chance of growing a third testicle than I do of becoming *rich* selling books. (However, the true story of a man who grew a third testicle *could* have a better chance than most in the non-fiction book marketplace. Titled *Awww, Nuts! The True Story of My Testicular Triumvirate,* the movie rights alone would make me rich.) So, aside from me dropping a third ball, there are many other surefire ways of becoming rich other than authoring a book: winning the lottery, ransomware, selling drugs, taking hostages, founding a pseudo-science religious cult—*anything* besides writing books. However, for the sake of argument, let's say I miraculously somehow manage to sell books. Subtracting the publisher's cut, agent fees, taxes, and payola, even if I sold like, *a million books,* I'd still make way less than a million dollars.

But let's put aside the impracticalities of getting rich as an *author* for a moment. Do you know how crazy-low the probability is of becoming a millionaire at *anything*? You should, because I told you in chapter 9. But here's another: according to the latest census data, only about one in a hundred Americans are millionaires. Maybe you think those are decent odds, but if you go into a restaurant and the waiter tells you there's a one in a hundred chance that the meal you are about to eat will have rat shit in it, I'm guessing you'd decide to pass on those odds and find another restaurant that offers the *zero chance* rat shit menu. So, barring gonad número tres, I'm tagging this definition as an ***improbability***.

As for the second part, *famous*??? How many famous authors are there? Really? Aside from Stephen King and J.K. Rowling, the only other author people know is Mother Goose.

And by the way, why is "being famous" always an automatic go-to for defining success? Does that mean if you're not a famous electrician or famous accountant or famous teacher you aren't successful at what you do? And what if you do become famous? Sure, you get free shit and everyone knows you, but you also get a lot of other crap you don't need or want, like stalkers and not being able to enjoy porno movies in a porno theatre.

Then there're people who're famous for something they don't want to be famous for. Like that guy whose wife hacked off his johnson—he's famous for his wife hacking off his johnson. Not sure how you parlay that into an endorsement deal. (Maybe somehow team up with a dude who has three testicles? I dunno.) Upon contemplating these probable scenarios, I have determined that fame is far too unpredictable to be a legitimate success-defining attribute. So, again, ***improbability***.

My second definition of success is a doozy: ***sex with a super-model***. At first glance, you might think this should be a defini-tion of *happiness*. But I'm pretty sure I could *never* be *happy* having sex with a supermodel. I mean, how could I? I'd be punching so goddamn far above my weight there'd be a Wiki page about it. Shit, the anxiety alone, knowing that everyone (including the supermodel) is looking at me, mouth agape, wondering *what the fuck is* she *doing with* him? would preclude any possibility of me enjoying myself. Not to mention, I'd have male supermodels, gods chiseled from hard slabs of masculinity, coming at me left and right to claim the supermodel goddess as their own. There'd be no way my soft and flabby, inadequate around-the-edges everyman incarnation could fend them off. The female supermodel would abandon me in a runway minute to be with her own kind. (And who would blame her? Not me). No, I love myself too much to do that to me. That's why I'll classify sex with a supermodel as a sign of *success*.

The success classification works especially well for me—a man in his late fifties, average in looks, physique, and intelligence with below-average ambition and financial means. With a supermodel on my arm, unless I'm wearing a top hat and a monocle, everyone would naturally assume that I must be wildly successful at *something* since a supermodel is having sex with me. We've all seen those much older, less attractive folks who've somehow managed to hook up with a far younger, more attractive, beau ideal. The only explanation for the delta is *success*. (Well, that and the inheritance short-game.) But, since I'm not that type of "successful," color this one an ***impossibility***.

Finally, definition number three: ***make people do my bidding***. Nothing says success more than other human beings acting upon my whims, making glorious exultation in service of my egoic edification. Alas, if I'm being honest with myself, this one's an ***improbability*** (not an *impossibility*). True, there are books that have inspired the masses to act in the author's interest. *Mein Kampf*, *The Bible*, *Dianetics*, and *The Art of the Deal* all come to mind. But the question I must ultimately ask myself is: *do I really want my book in the same category as Donald Trump's?* The answer is a decisive and divisive *hells to the no*. So, I guess I'll add ***conflict*** to this one as well.

All three of these definitions are long shots at best, making it highly unlikely even *one* of them will ever happen. So, by my own definitions, I'll never achieve success and will subsequently remain a miserable failure for the duration of my life.

Love

1. *Marriage*
2. *My own family*
3. *The adoration of others*

My first definition of *love* is **marriage**. Right out of the chute I'm off to a bad start. Here, I have fatuously linked my desire for a loving, committed, and enduring romantic relationship to matrimony. Do you see the problem here? I didn't. For as you may recall, I've already been married, and it didn't end well. I was left emotionally devastated, feeling unloved, unloving, and unlovable. Am I saying marriage is a "sham," a "racket," or a "no-win scenario?"

Not at all.

It's more like a game of Three-card Monte on a busy, big-city street corner. There are a lot of people gathered watching you bet on something you *think* you're gonna win at, when in actuality the other person's holding all the cards.

Don't get me wrong. I'm not saying I won't ever marry again. I have friends who are of great inspiration to me. They won't give up no matter how many times they fail to stick the landing. (Fifth time's a charm!) I'm just saying when the unpredictable, uncontrollable will of another free-thinking, independent person is involved in the situation, *I'm less likely to stake all my hopes of love on it.* Three-card Monte can be a lot of fun—so long as you never bet more than you can afford to lose. All of which I guess classifies marriage as a **conflict**.

Number two, **my own family (child/ren)**. This one's kind of part and parcel with the matrimony one—not completely, just… sorta. So, under common circumstances, this would've been a twofer. But for whatever reason I don't have any children (then again, I never answer my phone on Father's Day). Odd thing here is that I come from a close, loving family—mom, dad, and two younger brothers.

It was back in the 1970s and we actually did live in a *Brady Bunch* episode. Dad went to work, paid the bills, and was home at 5:00 p.m. and on weekends. Mom took care of the family, our suburban tract home, and was president of the PTA. I went to school and enjoyed extracurricular activities such as sports, Cub Scouts, and, eventually, dating. In other words, it was a totally fucked, hot mess of patriarchal oppression, misogynistic subjugation, and forced heterosexual & gender binary conformity, topped off with a heaping helping of systemic suburban racism. So, I naturally figured one day I too would have my own family.

Yet here I am in my late fifties, no wife, no kids, no suburban tract home. But even if I were to have a baby right now (I mean right *now*, as I write this), I'd be seventy-five years old when my child graduates high school. That's problematic to me. See, I had very young parents, and it was wonderful. Before I was age four, my mom introduced me to The Beatles with her *Revolver* album. My dad was agile and active enough to play sports with me and participate in my Scouting activities. I had the youngest, most active, and, I thought, coolest parents in our cul-de-sac. They listened to Burt Bacharach for Chrissake.

Now compare that to me as a dad: hobbling into my kids' parent-teacher conferences with my walker. The other parents mistaking me for my kids' grandfather. Belonging to the AARP rather than the PTA. Drooling more than my baby. Falling asleep before my kids do. And all that while they're still in *grade school*. By the time they reach high school, I'll need *them* to drive *me* around.

So, while I would not rate having a family at this time in my life as an impossibility, it is at least an ***improbability*** (and probably also a microaggression).

My third definition of love is **the adoration of others**. Yeah, so here's the problem with this one: adoration is like love but all amped up on sugar and coffee. *Oxford Languages* defines it as *worship; veneration*.

At first, that *seems* like a good idea. Who doesn't want people to worship *and* venerate them? But upon further examination, a wrinkle emerges, *feasibility*. It's a pretty big ask for others to worship and venerate you. I've had enough trouble just convincing people to have dinner with me. Now I have to somehow persuade them to *glorify* me too? The easiest way to do that is to be rich and famous or let everyone know you're having sex with a supermodel—both of which I've also pretty much vetoed. This one: ***Improbability***.

Comparing Across Categories

Conflicts, improbabilities, and ***impossibilities*** may also exist *across categories*. For example, one of my definitions of *success* is *sex with a supermodel*. Yet one of my definitions of *love* is *marriage*. Now, unless that supermodel is also my wife, I got me a genuine ***cross-category conflict*** (and likely an ***impossibility***).

As a measure of my *happiness*, I must have ***revenge on my enemies***. Yet in the *love* category, I want ***the adoration of others***. Again, I have a ***conflict*** and an ***impossibility***. There's no way my avowed enemies can adore me while my vengeance rains down upon them. So even if my heart is set on ***the adoration of others*** as a requirement for *love*, given this evaluation, I'll likely ax it in favor of ***revenge***. With my self-love now at an all-time high I don't need the adoration of others if it means giving up the satisfaction of punishing those who have betrayed me.

Let's Review…

Having completed an analysis of all nine definitions in all three categories, as well as an across-categories assessment, my annotated GRID looks like this (figure 16.1):

Figure 16.1

Eeeegh, what a mess! But you know the old saying: *You can't make a killing unless you get some blood on your hands.*

Now it's time for you to evaluate your definitions of **happiness, success,** and **love.** Remember, in this step, you're just *evaluating*—looking for **conflicts, improbabilities,** and **impossibilities.** You do *not* need to fix or redefine them—that's for later (besides, that would be far too much work for one step).

Oh, and one last pointer for this step. Really put some thought into it in an "anything isn't possible" kind of way while **having fun doing it!** (Actually, that was two last pointers—possibly three.) (And all in a very poorly constructed sentence.) Regardless, I'll be waiting for you in step 3 when you're finished.

CHAPTER 17
STEP 3: ALIGN YOUR RULES, VALUES, AND BELIEFS

If you don't stand for something you will fall for anything.
—Gordon A. Eadie

If I stand for too long, I fall anyway.
—M.K. Jackson

There's an old saying: a definition is only as strong as its weakest rules, values, and beliefs.

With that in mind, what were the results of the analysis of your definitions? Did you find *contradictions, improbabilities,* and *impossibilities*? My guess is you did. (And if for some reason you didn't—meaning you were already on your way to success, happiness, and love—don't even think about asking for a refund for this book.)

Assuming you *did* identify problems, fear not. I'm going to walk you through the fun and EZ process of converting them into definitions free of contradiction, improbability, and impossibility for your new happy, successful, and loving life.

But before we do, we'll take a quick break for a word from our sponsor: **new and improved *Rules, Values, and Beliefs...***

. . .

Your all-new rules, values, and beliefs are designed especially for you, by you, and with only your best interests in mind. So refreshingly different, they melt away those feelings of failure, misery, and loneliness, leaving you with the exhilarating sensation of authentic happiness, success, and love. Just one bite and you'll wonder how you ever lasted this long without them! Improved rules, values, and beliefs are part of a complete and fulfilling life. And now, back to the book.

Combined, our rules, values, and beliefs guide us morally, ethically, politically, spiritually, intellectually, and just about every other *ly* you can think of. With such a hefty responsibility in the direction of our lives, one would naturally assume they have been curated with great care and singular vision. But you know what they say happens when you assume, *you made that assumption using your rules, values, and beliefs.*

Step 3 is creating a new set of rules, values, and beliefs that eradicate all the contradictions, improbabilities, and impossibilities in your current definitions of success, happiness, and love. Just what makes this new set so effective where the previous ones were not? *Personalization.* We're going to build them from the ground up to reflect *your* best interests, advance *your* agenda, and make all *your* dreams come true!* Oh, it's going to be so perfect in every way that you'll feel all warm and gooey inside, like when your pants are full of warmed tapioca pudding. And best of all, it's EZ and takes little effort.

Before we proceed, let's take a moment and review what rules, values, and beliefs are in the context of this book.

Rules (which include laws) are black and white. Right or wrong. Little-to-no wiggle room and not much latitude for inter-

---

* The definition of "dreams" is based upon happiness, success, and love as defined in this book. "Coming true" is determined by a subjective assessment and therefore may differ depending upon the sample. Individual results may vary from person to person based on the type of dream, the quantity of dreams, and other factors including your age, lifestyle, and expectations.

pretation. More often than not we don't create our own rules (and *that's* the problem), they're taught to (*imposed* on us is more like it) by institutions (family, school, church) to protect and promote their own designs and purposes.

The United States Constitution, the Bible, and *Star Trek's* Prime Directive are all jam-packed with a bunch of rules and laws to boss you around and keep you in line personally, morally, societally, and when exploring the galaxy. Arguably the most successful of all rules and laws are God's *Ten Commandments*, ten rules all packaged together that debuted at number one with a bullet and have charted for over 2,700 years. (Not to mention they were introduced in the best-selling book of all time and they've had not one but *two* titular major motion pictures made about them—one of them starring Charlton Fucking Heston. Take *that*, U.S. Constitution.)

Values are the most personal of the three. They are the moral and ethical compass that make up our standards of behavior. Generally speaking, we adopt the values we were raised with— but not always or all ways. While primarily formed by religious and spiritual affiliations they are also shaped by society, culture, and community. Since values are our fundamental principles, they often hold greater sway over our thoughts and actions than even rules and beliefs.

Beliefs are contextual and subjective—your beliefs are yours and yours alone (however, others may hold the same beliefs as you and vice versa). You can *believe* in the craziest shit in the world—ghosts, UFOs, religion, the American Dream—without having to prove it or have it proven, just so long as you *believe* it.

Beliefs are formed by our knowledge and experience both of which are fluid. As we learn, or *un*learn, our beliefs can shift. For this reason, between the three, beliefs change the most, and changing them can be easiest—depending, that is, upon how crazy the shit is that you believe.

. . .

Rules, Values, and Beliefs Working In Tandem Against Us

When I was a child, I believed in Santa Claus. My rules and values were solely dedicated to being "good" all year—telling the truth, acting respectfully, not swearing, not masturbating—just so I could get toys at Christmas time. But that belief changed in my twenties when I learned there was no such thing as Santa Claus. I came to understand that my parents used that belief against me to manipulate my behavior. Their childhood model of living a never-say-lies, respect-filled, obscenity-bereft, anti-masturbatory life 364 days a year for one lousy pay-off on the 365th is no longer sustainable. As an adult, those forced behaviors became obstacles to my happiness, success, and love. Seriously NO lies—every day??? C'mon. Who does that?

I'm now in the twilight of my life and have too few remaining years to waste on someone else's rules, values, and beliefs. (Especially if it means no more jerkin' the gherkin. C'mon. Who doesn't do that?)

The System Is Rigged Against You and You're the Only One Who Can Unrig It

While most of our flawed rules, values, and beliefs were shaped by outside incongruous influence, those we've formed on our own, especially later in life, can be just as malignant. We may *think* we created them independently of others, but more likely, we unwittingly adopted them through the poisoned perspectives of our current rules, values, and beliefs—like a Xerox of a Xerox of a Xerox.* Some may have been forged as personal defense mechanisms we subconsciously constructed to

---

* For those not of the analog perversion, Xerox is a company that began manufacturing machines in 1959 that, to this day, make paper copies of paper documents. Unlike digital files, each subsequent paper copy of the document or the user's ass (the genericization of which is a "Xerox") decreases in visual integr—OH FOR FUCK SAKE! I'm not gonna explain what a goddamned Xerox is!

protect ourselves from physical, psychological, and/or emotional vulnerability.

Admittedly, sometimes through the grace of God or mere happenstance (depending on your rules, values, and beliefs), this haphazard patchwork miraculously aligns with our pursuit of happiness, success, and love. But mostly, I've painfully discovered, not so much. But despair not for all is not lost!

A wonderful thing about rules, values, and beliefs is they are *updatable*—just like the operating system of your phone or computer. In fact, for the purposes of step 3, think of your rules, values, and beliefs as just that: *your* operating system—the interface managing the allocation of resources for your happiness, success, and love.

In this step, you're going to create a *Rules, Values, and Beliefs List* so you can isolate and eliminate the corrupt files shitting all over your happiness, success, and love. Then, you'll update them with a new system that operates in *your* best interests.

WARNING! EFFORT ALERT!
The following section involves thinking and writing. A modicum of time and effort on the part of you, the reader, will be required.

To ensure maximum benefit with minimal effort, please remember to follow these three rules:

1. Use a *single* piece of paper for the lessercise—more pages = more work.
2. Do *not* use a computer for the lessercises—embrace the *Three Ps*: paper, pencil, pen.
3. Do *not* overthink the lessercises—overthinking is overrated.

Keep it simple—Keep it analog.™

ADDITIONAL WARNING!
Journaling Alert!

When undertaking this second lessercise, you will likely be inclined to use *another* piece of paper. DO NOT do this! Multiple pages assembled in service of a singular theme, subject, or purpose brings you dangerously close to journaling. To avoid this hazard, it is imperative you *use the back page of your step 2 grid*.

To begin, simply list the three header categories: *Happiness, Success,* and *Love.* Below each of the three headers, write *Current Rule, New Rule; Current Value, New Value; Current Belief, New Belief,* each on its own line.

Your *Rules, Values, and Beliefs List* should look like this (figure 17.1):

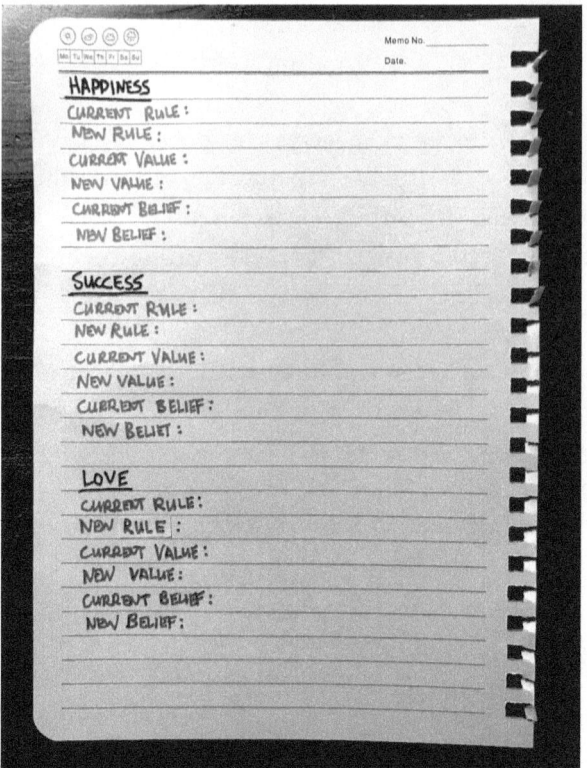

Figure 17.1

Now write down one current *rule*, one current *value*, and one current *belief* you have for *happiness* and *success* and *love*—that's a total of nine writing down things (that's the best I can word it).

You likely have several rules, values, and beliefs for each, but just go with your top *one*—and don't spend a lot of time *thinking* about them. Go with whatever first pops into your head for each category. More often than not, that'll be the truest answer and give us the real reason you're subconsciously ruining your life. Oh, and don't write down answers you think are "right" or make you look good—that defeats the purpose. Honesty is the best policy—no matter how fucked up you are.

For instance, as a rule, do you think happiness must be *earned* or is it yours for the taking? Do you *believe* you *deserve* to be happy? Is happiness a *birthright*? Do you value it enough to *strive* for it or is it within you already?

Is your *rule* for *success* a specific *job,* or a corner *office,* or a specific amount of *money,* or a particular job with a corner office making a specific amount of money? How much do you *value* success? Does it define your value as a *person*? Or do *you* define *it*? Do you believe to be successful you must *be the best*? Or must you *do your best*?

Does your rule for love in your life protect you from it or open you to it? How much do you *value love*? Is it *necessary* in your life? Transcendent? *Transactional*? *Transient*? Do you believe you are *worthy* of love? Is it worthy of you?

To offer you some guidance, here are my (previously) current rules, values, and beliefs for happiness, success, and love (figure 17.2):

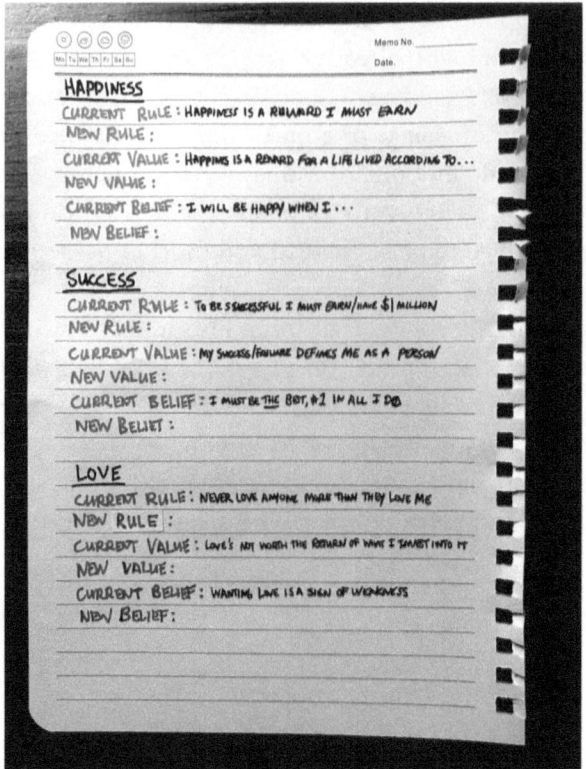

Figure 17.2

Now it's your turn. Go ahead and write down your current rule, value, and, belief for happiness, success, and love. When you're finished, I'll be right here waiting for you.

.

.

.

Welcome back and well done! Were you surprised by any of your answers? Did you discover any blaring or glaring conflicts or disconnects? If you're not sure, you're about to find out.

The process of (re)aligning your rules, values, and beliefs begins with assessing each of these current ones and isolating those that sabotage your success, happiness, and love. But how do you identify the saboteurs? Well, I've made finding the recreants easier than you may think with the **seven positive traits** and **four negative traits** your rules, values, and beliefs ~~should~~ must have...

Positive Traits

Each of your rules, values, and beliefs **must** contain *all* the following qualities (okay maybe not every one of them, but certainly the more the better):

1. *Mediocrity.* Do I really need to remind you of this? Being happy, successful, or in love has *nothing* to do with "excellence," "the best," or "trying." *Aim for the middle, that's where the bullseye is.*

2. **Vague; non-committal.** (i.e., un*trackable*.) The *worst* thing you can do is commit—to *anything*. Keep things amorphous and you keep them manageable. Use my example of arrival time: if you tell someone you'll pick them up at 7:00 p.m., every minute you're late is another minute that person grows angrier at your "tardiness." By the time you arrive a mere twenty minutes "late," the evening is ruined because they're so pissed at your "unpunctuality." Do as I do and tell them you'll be there between 7:00 and 8:00 p.m. That way you have set a realistic expectation that you are sure to meet. By the time you arrive fifteen, thirty, or even forty-five minutes in, you're still "on time." Everyone's happy and the evening is a success.

3. **Reflects your ethics, morals, and convictions.** Since you're reading this book, I'm guessing you're an adult (I don't think schools even teach kids to read anymore —just how to use emojis), and since that's the case, you are no longer that person from decades ago whose character was shaped more by others than yourself. You're a big {gender identification} now. Take charge

of your life and destiny (just don't try so hard
doing it).

4. **Serves *your* agendas and interests first and foremost.**
   If all those other people and institutions in your life
   want their rules, values, and beliefs adopted to serve
   their agendas, then let *them* read this fucking book and
   do the work.

5. **Will *not* cause ill will or harm to yourself or others.**
   Mediocrity and stacking the deck doesn't mean you
   have to be a prick. Keep your karmic clock clean.

6. **Works in unity with all your other rules, values, and
   beliefs**—no conflicts or contradictions. You cannot
   value being healthy while making it a rule to eat a
   daily diet of delicious fried foods while believing
   exercise is a hoax (as I do).

7. **The path of least resistance is the easiest road
   traveled.** Your rules, values, and beliefs must map out
   the shortest, least obstructed path to your definitions
   of happiness, success, and love. This means no lofty,
   overreaching, or needlessly redemptive blanket
   aspirations buried within them—things like valuing
   excessive accountability, believing it's always better to
   give than receive, or automatically ruling out easy
   work. This is not religion, you don't get extra points
   for making life harder on yourself.

Negative Traits

Each of your rules, values, and beliefs **must not** contain any
of these attributes:

1. **Outdated.** After being repeatedly victimized by the
   points in this book endlessly and mercilessly
   sledgehammered home, it is hoped that you have

developed the ability to discern anything and everything in your life that's useless in your mediocric drive toward happiness, success, and love. This obviously includes any previously installed inefficacious rules, values, and beliefs you may still possess. It's like that coffee mug with the broken handle you kept for sentimental reasons or reusing that same condom because rubber's a non-biodegradable waste product and you want to "save" the environment. A thing without a use is a useless thing. Throw that shit out and get a new one that *works*.

2. **Detail.** (i.e., *trackable.*) Specificity is the silent killer of dreams. Once you back yourself into a corner with promises to deliver, you've already decreased your chances for happiness, success, and love by at least 50 percent—usually more—because commitment is the yardstick with which to measure failure, misery, and loneliness.

3. **Used only because of its origin.** Just because someone close to you (family, friends, significant other), an authority figure (parents, politician, clergy), a person you admire (hero, idol), or an institution (civic, religious, academic) instilled the rule, value, or belief in you that doesn't mean it's in *your* best interests. If it ain't, shitcan it.

4. (This goes without saying, so I'll *write* it) **Violates laws, commandments, or other regulations**—especially when it can result in harm (including death) to yourself or others. This includes your own incarceration. For example, your definition of being a successful serial killer is to murder as many people as possible and you made a new rule that killing is okay. Don't do that. Any rule, value, or belief proclaiming murder to be good is bad and your problems likely

run deeper than definitions of happiness, success, and love. In which case I'm in way over my head with this book and you need to seek professional help.

Seriously. My lawyer assures me I am not joking here.

After having applied these lists of positive and negative traits to your current rules, values, and beliefs (as well as everything else you've gathered thus far from this book), you are ready to suss out which ones can stay (if any) and which ones need to go (I'm guessing many).

Rewriting the Rules (and Values and Beliefs)

A major highlight when attending my *Reaching the Heights of Your Potential by Plumbing the Depths of Mediocrity* online master-class is the "Fucked by Your Own Rules, Values, and Beliefs" workshop. I walk each attendee through the evaluation of their rules, values, and beliefs, pinpointing the ones that torpedo their happiness, success, and love. I then assist each person in realigning their obstructive rules, values, and beliefs into a new, empowering foundation for happiness, success, and love.

But given this is a book and I have no idea what the hell you came up with, the best I can offer here and now is to share with you *my* old rules, values, and beliefs alongside my realigned ones and outline the methodology that got me there as guidance in your process.

HAPPINESS

I thought a lot about the origins of my happiness—what allowed it as well as what denied it. More often than not it fell under the purview of some religious, moral, or ethical authority (I was raised Catholic, after all).

Usually, these types of sectarian institutions lord the promise of everlasting happiness, or eternal suffering, over us as a bargaining chip so we act and behave in specific ways, believe in certain things, and sell our soul to the company store.

My major breakthrough in refuting this came when I accepted that happiness is not managed by an outside source, but rather cultivated from a source from within—myself. (That and there's no such place as hell... no matter how much I masturbate.)

My current happiness rule: *Happiness is a reward I have to earn.*

Evaluation: WRONG! Happiness is not a paycheck, it's a birthright. And thinking otherwise is just narcissistic, self-indulgent, pity party-throwing martyrdom.

My new happiness rule: *I can be as happy as I decide to be.*

Realignment: Former president Abe Lincoln said that, so you know it's true.* The brilliance of this rule is that it gives *me*, not *others*, the power over my happiness. While it's admittedly more difficult than not, I can indeed be happy with the one simple decision to be so. I know things will happen in life that prevent me from being happy 24/7, but if I'm not taking responsibility for my happiness, then I'm taking accountability for my misery.

When my wife and I separated I was pretty fucking far from being happy. It went on for months. Every day, no smiling, no laughing, no hope, a pit in my stomach. Over time I became exhausted from being so unhappy. It was at that point something interesting began to happen... Just the very state of being so unhappy became more of an emotional burden than the actual reason I wasn't happy to begin with. I didn't miss my wife any less, I just hated being unhappy more.

---

* While this quote is often attributed to Honest Abe (especially by the self-help industrial complex), the website Quote Investigator concludes: "... there is no substantive evidence that Abraham Lincoln used this expression. It was attributed to him by Dr. Frank Crane about fifty years after his [Lincoln] death... The popularity of the saying was enhanced by its appearance in the perennial self-help blockbuster *How to Win Friends and Influence People* by Dale Carnegie where it was ascribed to Lincoln."

That was the impetus for my conscious decision to be happy. My rediscovered happiness wasn't a switch I could just flick on. Nothing outside of me changed. I was still divorced, my wife was still gone, and I was still alone. Yet *deciding* to be happy again was the all-important first step because it changed my mindset and my perspective. There was now *the hope* I could be happy—the balls were in my lap.

My current happiness value: *Being happy is a reward, for a life lived according to {insert any religious, cultural, political, moral, ethical, et al ethos foisted upon you by a secondary source of authority}.*

Evaluation: Again, WRONG! I don't have to wait for anyone to give me permission to be happy, least of all some bullshit transactional plan set up by someone else so I follow their agenda.

My new happiness value: *True happiness comes from within.*

Realignment: I know, I know, it's hella cliché—but it's also true (which is why it's a cliché). (Just like saying "the reason it's a cliché is because it's true" is also a cliché.)

When my house is cold, I don't warm myself by heating the outside to recreate the effects of a hot day. I heat the inside where it's manageable. Acknowledging that my happiness comes from within me where only I can access it, I eliminate any outside power determining my happiness.

Even when I think something or someone is making me happy, it isn't, and they aren't. That's because my happiness is based on causation, the capacity of which I define. I alone permit that specific thing or certain person to make me happy. Therefore, it follows that I can also determine whether a thing or person is *not* necessary to make me happy. Taking this premise a step further, I can even remove the power from something or someone to make me *un*happy. Unless I am literally imprisoned and physically deprived of my liberty, I hold the power over my happiness and unhappiness. And even then, it's still up to me. But that's a whole different level, one I'm not on—and one for a different book. (Which has already been written by Viktor Frankl.)

My current happiness belief: *I will be happy when I get "{PER-SON(S):PLACE(S):THING(S)}"*

Evaluation: As I just stated, persons, places, and things are out of my control. They can be given and taken at will (a will not my own). It's antithetical to common sense *and* a happy life to give anything that precarious power over my happiness. *Contribute* to it? Sure. But not control it.

My new happiness belief: *Happiness is my birthright.*

Realignment: To paraphrase Tommy Jefferson:

*[Everyone is] endowed. And that's something to be happy about, especially when it's by the Creator with certain unalienable Rights, that among these are Life, Liberty, and the pursuit of **Happiness**.* There you go. Right there in the Declaration of Independence, the word *happiness* with a capital "H." And that, dear reader, is why the United States of America is the greatest goddamned country in the history of the universe times infinity: it's our unalienable *right* to be happy.* (Which also includes our *God-given* right to carry a loaded pistol.)

The important distinction here is that happiness is not like building a pergola in your backyard. You don't need a permit from the city government to do it; it's handled by the federal government (your happiness, not the pergola).

SUCCESS

Of the three categories, *success* is the one that previously eluded me most. It's the one with which I had the most contentious relationship and the most unfulfilling. I suspect this may be true for many people.

---

* If you are not a United Statesian and you're reading this book, don't worry. It's also *your* birthright to be happy. Apparently, you too are under the same jurisdiction of the authority from which the Declaration of Independence derives its just powers.

The tricky thing about success is that its meaning so widely varies—culturally, philosophically, emotionally, materially, mentally, and mathematically.

I had so many disparate determinators of success stuffed into my brain from as many sources that I could never accomplish any of them.

It wasn't until I established my own personal rules, values, and beliefs toward success that I could finally define what it meant to me and move closer to attaining it.

My current success rule: *To be successful I must earn $1 million a year or more.*

Evaluation: Waaaaay too specific. It's that ol' "one million dollars" stock answer to be "successful" popping up again. Says who? And why? With inflation, recession, and depression how much is a million bucks really worth in today's world anyway? Post-taxes, I'd be lucky to live off a million for three years. Then it's back to being a failure again. Yay.

But far more damaging is there's no wiggle room in this rule. With such specificity, anything less than a million Washingtons qualifies as a bona fide failure. So if I earn $999,999.99 I'm unsuccessful? Well, it *is* specifically less than a million bucks, so yes, I'm unsuccessful. Man, that is messed up. And that's the trouble with specificity.

My new success rule: *Success is having done my best at something.*

Realignment: While writing this, I looked up the word success in the thesaurus. Here are some of the synonyms: *profitable, moneymaking, lucrative, solvent,* and *bankable.*

Are those the only things to be valued as success? Is a volunteer at the animal shelter who cares for and saves neglected pets a failure because they didn't make any money doing it? Or could they be deemed successful because the results of their actions had a positive effect?

When you know the answer to that, you know that success truly has nothing to do with emoluments. However, fear not, ye of the materially inclined (of whom I consider myself to be a proud, card-carrying member). This value leaves open the option of desiring and acquiring material objects, including money and things. It just doesn't make them the determining factor in success.

Despite this book, I still want to be a successful author. So, for the hell of it, I looked up the definition of the word *author* in *three* different sources…

author
1: the writer of a literary work (such as a book).
2: one that originates or creates something.[1]

author
1: the writer of a book, article, play, etc.
2: a person who begins or creates something.[2]

author
1: a person who writes a novel, poem, essay, etc.; the composer of a literary work, as distinguished from a compiler, translator, editor, or copyist.
2: the literary production or productions of a writer.
3: the maker of anything; creator; originator.[3]

Merriam-Webster, Cambridge, and Dictionary.com. Not a goddamn one of them includes remuneration in their definition of an author. They use action verbs like *writing, creating, composing, originating,* and *making,* but not *earning.* Therefore, to be an author, I've decided I just need to write. And if I simply finish this book, whether I get paid or not, I will indeed be a *successful* author—maybe not a *professional* author, but an author nonetheless.

I'm not oblivious to the reality that I need legal tender to pay my mortgage and bills and to enjoy myself. That's why I have a job. I take pride in my work, and I apply myself, doing the best I can. But the fact is my job as a project manager exists outside of my abilities. The job evolves. The job changes. The job demands what it needs regardless of what I'm able to do. And should the job's demands exceed my capacity, I'll be fired.

But if I did the best I could, given who I am with the skills and abilities I possess, then I'll see myself as a successful author who simply couldn't manage other people's projects and must now look for a different way to earn a living.

My current success value: *My success and/or failure define me as a person.*

Evaluation: Too vague—and too much pressure. My success or failure only defines my success or failure—nothing more. This is hella true especially because the definitions we most often use are completely uninformed, unrelated, and unproductive to our own situations. Man, I could not wait to realign this one because this old value omits what it is that I personally *actually* value as "success."

My new success value: *I define my success (and failure).*

Realignment: I think this one's self-obvious. The ol' switcharoo. I've come to learn in my over half-century living in the Thunderdome that when a rule, value, or belief proves to be fallacious, I can usually de-fallate it by reversing it on itself.

I alone have the power and authority to decide what defines my success or failure in any given circumstance. For everything in my life—writing, friendships, love, and yes, even my job—I define success by my commitment, personal satisfaction, learning, growth, and the treatment of others (by me and to me)—or why the fuck am I even doing it? Just for the money?

Look: I know I'm living on borrowed time. My father and both my grandfathers didn't live to see sixty. My day died at *fifty-four* and his dad at *forty-seven*. So I totally get it: I'm driving through life on an expired license. Any minute now I'm gonna see red lights in my rearview mirror and the devil's gonna pull me over—and it won't be to give me a fix-it ticket. So for me, *time* is the most precious commodity. This is baked into my DNA and subsequently my perspective on *failure*—chiefly, I'm not afraid of it.

There are three things to never fear:

1. Don't fear the walking dead.
2. Don't fear the Reaper.
3. Don't fear failure.

I know that virtually nothing ever created of merit, significance, or endurance got it right on the first shot. And even though we failed to land on the moon, we did get Velcro, Tang, and a great movie quote* for the effort. So, we didn't really fail, did we? Remember: *If at first you don't succeed, try try, but not too hard, again.*

My current success belief: *I must be the very best, #1, in everything I do to be successful.*

Evaluation: The best? #1? And at *every goddamned thing*??? We've already gone over what the odds are at being the #1 best at *anything*. All that does is put unnecessary, undue, unrealistic, and unachievable pressure on me. I am now convinced that I can be successful in being #46,933 at something.

My new success belief: *As long as I do my very best, I am successful.*

Realignment: How brilliant is this? Come what may, this allows me, not others, to define my success. This is important because a comparison to others to determine my own success at anything is a fatal path to surefire failure on someone else's terms.

It would be great to be as amazing a writer as {insert favorite author} and I can still aspire to it. But it can't be the only yardstick by which I measure my success because there'll always be someone better.

---

* *Houston, we have a problem.* How many times have you said that when something fucked up?

Are Herman's Hermits better than the Beatles? Arguably not. But Herman's Hermits did enjoy success by doing the best they could. Sure, I want to be a Beatle, but frankly, I'm more a Herman's Hermit.

LOVE

Ugh... Of the three categories, my rules, values, and beliefs regarding love are the most screwed up—and I'm the one primarily responsible for screwing 'em. Upon examination, I discovered a reactionary approach in their design and purpose meant to compensate for my lack of self-love and/or protect myself from future heartbreak.

Either way, my attempts to supplant emotional vulnerability with no-risk romantic involvement left me hanging alone, choked out by autoneurotic asphyxiation.

My current love rule: *Never love anyone more than they love me.*

Evaluation: I'm all for stacking the deck in favor of my emotional protection, but all this does is create an emotional standoff between two people (or more... I'm open to it) waiting for the other to dive in first. The origin of this rule is my need to play it safe—like locking a door to keep all the scary things outside. But you know, all that really does is keep me locked up all alone, isolated from everyone else. (Now that I see this one in writing, I'm not so sure it makes as much sense as I thought it did when I was thinking it.)

My new love rule: *Love myself irrespective of what others do.*

Realignment: With my current (old) rule, I cut myself off from fully investing in love because someone might reject me. And so what if they do? So fucking what? Since when does my worthiness to be loved have to be co-signed? Why deprive myself of a glorious emotional experience that could last the rest of my life, let alone the rest of the night? Because I'm afraid of rejection? Why should someone else's rejection of me be stronger than my acceptance of myself? Nothing in life worth having comes risk-free.

And I'll tell you something else: at this point in my life, with all the shit that I've had to deal with, the least of my fucking fears is someone *rejecting* me. Really? That's the worst you got? My dad's dead. My mom's dead. My cat's dead. My second cat's dead. I survived a divorce, a layoff, a pandemic, two brain surgeries, and five radiation treatments to my head. GOD ALMIGHTY couldn't take me out—you think a fucking rejection slip's gonna do it?

So, rather than trying in vain to eliminate the risk (which is sooooo never gonna happen), I removed my *reaction* to the risk. My new rule resolves the old one by shifting the responsibility of my feeling loved and worthy from others onto myself—where it belongs.

My current love value: *Love is not worth the minuscule return on its arduous investment.*

Evaluation: Another unfounded attempt to protect me from being hurt by love that actually prevents me from having it. This old value frames love as a transactional arrangement with built-in expectations for reciprocation. As a defense mechanism against future investments, I became *The Love Accountant.* Using my score sheet, I added and subtracted the gains and losses from every failed relationship. Then, unable to balance the books, I just wrote off my entire love life before it wrote me off. And that, my dudes, is fucked up. *

My new love value: *Love is like the universe… it's infinite.*

Realignment: When anything is seen to be finite the stakes seem higher. My new value removes the scarcity principle so now love is abundant. I simply switched the equation around so

---

* This, by the way, is not a bad idea for a movie or limited series. *"The Love Accountant,* a Quinn Martin production." All these guest stars appear as The Love Accountant's clients who reconcile their toxic relationships through manipulative psychology, emotional transactions, and killer spreadsheets. I'd watch that shit.

no matter the "investment," there's always a high "dividend" yield. It's simple loveonomics.

My current love belief: *Wanting love is a sign of weakness.*

Evaluation: Another smoke screen to protect me from being rejected or hurt—and frankly, from not having it.

My new love belief: *Giving and accepting love is a sign of strength.*

Realignment: What I've learned about love (and it's not much) is that it's not about weakness, it's about vulnerability. I conflated the two. I was wrong. In love, the willingness to be vulnerable is essential. With vulnerability comes authenticity, trust, and the courage to risk being hurt so that the relationship can grow. In love, when your guard is up, your chances of finding it go down. That's simple loveonomics.

Having completed all my new rules, values, and beliefs for happiness, success, and love, here is what my list looks like (figure 17.3):

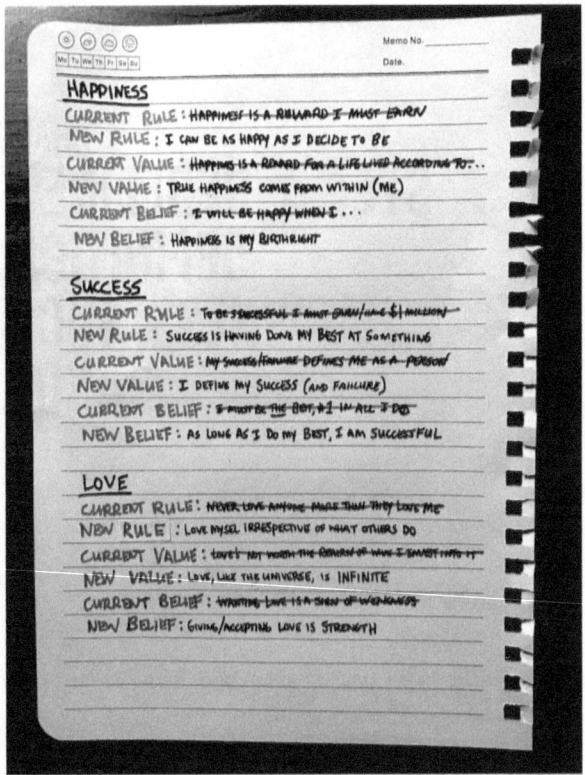

Figure 17.3

It's Better to Do It Write than to Just Get It Done

It's time for you to create *your* new rules, values, and beliefs. Take as much time as you need. (Well, not "as much as you need." I mean, don't take, like, a year.)

Put some serious thought into it. These new rules, values, and beliefs are going to be the foundation for your future happiness, success, and love.

When you're finished, meet me in "Step 4: Redefining Your Defining of Success, Happiness, and Love" where we'll *finally* put all this to bed.

CHAPTER 18

STEP 4: REDEFINE YOUR DEFINITIONS OF HAPPINESS, SUCCESS, AND LOVE

We cannot solve our problems with the same thinking we used when we created them.

—Albert Einstein

Hey, Einstein, then maybe you should stop thinking so much since it's creating problems. For Chrissake, you're supposed to be the genius here.

—M.K. Jackson

People often forget that in the movie *Rocky* (the first and good one) Rocky Balboa did *not* win the fight. His opponent, heavyweight champion Apollo Creed, won by split decision.

Yet, at the end of the movie, when the match was over, the music was triumphant, Rocky looked victorious as he embraced his girlfriend Adrian, and we, the audience, lost our shit, cheering, screaming, and jumping around the theatre as if *we* just won the fight. But WHY? Our guy *lost*.

How did this movie jerk us off for two hours then edge us with Rocky *losing*, and still deliver a happy ending?

The answer is obvious (if you read the title of this section),

Rocky applied *Step 4: Redefine Your Definitions of Happiness, Success, and Love.*

Rocky was, in fact, a *mediocre* fighter. A ham and egger who slugged it out in small clubs while working as a collector for a loan shark to supplement his income. He knew he could not stand toe-to-toe with Creed who was the superior boxer in every regard—skill, experience, mustache, poise, and showmanship.

The night before the fight, as he lay next to his girlfriend Adrian, Rocky calmly told her:

"All I want to do is go the distance. Nobody's ever gone the distance with Creed. And if I can go that distance... I'm gonna know for the first time in my life, see? That I weren't just another bum from the neighborhood."

By pretty much every metric, success in a title fight is *winning* the fight. In boxing, there is no second place—it's called *losing*. But Rocky *redefined* his definition of success. He lowered his sights from winning the match (something he knew he could *not* do) to going the full fifteen rounds (something he knew he could *maybe* do). Kobayashi Maru.

But faaaaaar more important here is that Rocky wasn't just trying to find a loophole or a way to justify losing the fight. Nor was he preserving his $150,000 payday (around $800,000 in today's dollars). Rocky redefined success *to* his *rules, values, and beliefs*. More than winning or losing, Rocky valued his self-respect.

By being the first fighter to go the full fifteen rounds against Creed, Rocky wouldn't be "just another bum from the neighborhood." With success now on Rocky's terms—aligned with his rules, values, and beliefs—it meant something profound to him at a *personal* level. And that's the secret to step 4.

The movie's exhilarating ending, record box office (making 225.0 times its production budget[1]), Academy Awards (including Best Picture), and permanent place in cinema history (including the theme music that's been used in every goddamn training sequence ever since—both real and reel) all proved *Rocky* right:

sometimes it's not about winning, it's about going the distance. Better to drink some raw eggs, pump out a few one-armers, beat the meat, and call it a draw.

For Rocky and you, step 4 is the final stage in creating your happy, successful, and loving life. By using your newly minted rules, values, and beliefs along with all the other tools in this book (including not trying so hard, making whiskey sours, and mediocrity), you will *redefine* happiness, success, and love in ways that are attainable, actionable, and ultimately benefitable.

Like everything else in my life that I've already said, I'll say it again: this book is *not* an anti-materialism manifesto. I love materialism, I myself have lots of materials including some stupid, crazy-ass shit I kept from my childhood and collected over the years all of which makes me feel very happy and/or successful: my townhouse, vintage Brasilia furniture, Don Draper's coffee pot (an *authentic* prop from *Mad Men*), unopened/on-the-card vintage 12-back Darth Vader and 21-back Boba Fett *Star Wars* action figures (I was a real anal retent as a kid), an assortment of 60s character cereal spoons (Tony the Tiger, Yogi Bear, Huckleberry Hound, et al.), and a large collection of spirit/talking (Ouija) boards. Given the success of my material accumulation, I encourage you to accumulate as many materials as your heart desires. They can indeed add quality and joy to life—they have for me.

However, there is one caveat to all those wonderful material and nonmaterial objects being the *sole* mainspring of happiness and success. Don't worry—I'm NOT gonna lay some high-fructose corn syrup greeting card/Instagram post cliché on you like *Happiness doesn't result from what we get, but from what we give.* And it's not just because that hacky adduce of derivation is from Ben Carson (yes, *that* Ben Carson). No, I wouldn't tell you that because it's bullshit. Believe you me, I know this from personal experience. I've tried that whole "giving" thing and it's rarely what it's cracked up to be—especially when I'm the only one giving (which is often the case). Might as well change the quote to *Being a chump doesn't result from when we get, but from when we do all the giving* (which is actually a pretty good quote, making me smarter than Ben Carson). But that has nothing at all to do with this step, section, or paragraph. So rather than suggest you perform such an improvident act of self-immolation at the altar of altruism, I'm gonna lay *this* quote on you instead...

> *Our abode in this world is transitory, our life therein is but a loan, our breaths are numbered and our indolence is manifest.*
> —Abu Bakr

Take *that* optimism. I have that quote taped to my bathroom mirror, my bedroom mirror, my rearview mirror, and my two-way mirror—that's how true and important I believe that quote to be. Especially the "indolence is manifest" part. *Fucking brilliant.*

See, what I've learned thus far from my adventure called "life" is two-fold. First, the British use different words than Americans for the same thing. Ridiculously nonsensical words like "snog" for *kiss* and "crisps" for *potato chips.* So why not just call them *chips* like normal people? Well, because in a tectonic perversion of all logical rationality, "chips" to the Brits are what we call *french fries,* which is all the more "barmy" (the British word for *crazy in nature* WTF?) because french fries come from the words pommes frites. And in French, *pomme de terre* means *potato,* and *frites* means *fries.* Put them together, and it's literally FRENCH FRIES!

The second thing I've "learnt" (that's the British English past tense of *learned*—all screwy) is that the nature of things, *every*things—people, places, and things—is transitory. Nothing lasts for long (let alone forever).* *Knowing* and *accepting* the tran-

---

* Actually, that's not entirely true. Herpes last forever. At least that's what

sitory nature of life is like taking a self-empowerment laxative, you'll be shitting happiness, success, and love.

The Transitory Nature of an Ice Cube

An ice cube is one of the most versatile tools known to humans. It keeps your whiskey cold, relieves burns, dewrinkles your clothes, waters plants, fights pimples, prevents sauces from curdling, smooths caulk seams, reduces bruises, eases splinter removal, brings the swelling down on your groin, cleans garbage disposals, and takes chewing gum out of carpets. When you first get a new ice cube, it's dry, shiny, and cool. Yet eventually, that ice cube will melt away. It will be gone and you'll be forced to handle your groin on your own.

But it's because you know the nature of ice is transitory—it will eventually melt away—you are not emotionally traumatized when an ice cube is gone. You expect it so you accept it.

To put this concept into a more personal, practical application, say my entire Ouija board collection is stolen. I'd (eventually) be okay with it because I no longer predicate my success and happiness on *things*.

Of course, I'd miss them and I'd want them back. But I'd be just as happy without them as I was with them because it's illogical and irresponsible to base my happiness on them when the nature of all things is transitory. Nothing lasts forever.

(Plus, I'd be okay with it because I'd find satisfaction in unleashing the legion of tortured spirits captured within the boards to possess and haunt the son of a bastard who stole them. Revenge is a dish best served through a portal to the demonic realm.)

---

someone told me.

Way back in chapter 3, I shared with you my original list of what I thought would've made me happy, successful, and loved:

- a well-paying "real" job w/benefits;
- marriage;
- one year's living expenses;
- physical and mental health;
- spiritual harmony;
- *blah-blah-blah, quack-quack-quack.*

When I attained these things (some more than others) I did indeed feel happy, successful, and in love.

But the problem wasn't how I felt having them; it was how I felt after losing them. When I was unemployed, divorced, had a brain tumor, was still not a homeowner, and my savings had dwindled. Just like that: bruiser to loser. I no longer felt happy, successful, or loved.

It wasn't that all those things on my list weren't worthy of pursuit. It's that I gave them too much say-so in defining my happiness, success, and love. I never considered their transitory nature so when they melted away it sent me into a two-year tailspin. Having lived through that depression-filled, self-loathing, dark time, if something is now going to have that much control over my life, I want to at least have a say in the approval process. Wouldn't you?

Success, the Problem Child Sibling of Happiness and Love

How would you describe *happiness*? Feeling carefree? Content? Euphoric?

How would you describe love/being in *love*? Blissful? Invincible? Vulnerable?

How would you describe *success*? Graduating first in your class? Having a well-paid, respected career? A corner office? A specific dollar amount? A hella cool car?

Did you notice anything different about describing success compared to happiness and love...? I'll give you a moment to think about it...

.

.

.

While we normally define happiness and love with *feelings* and *emotions*, most often, we define success with *things*. In our blended family of happiness, success, and love, *success* is the problem child—you know, the one that's extra difficult and a lot more work than the others but is ultimately still worth keeping. We shower *success* with *things*, but what it really needs from us is more *emotion*, so it feels as important as its brother and sister.

Now admittedly, I'm painting in broad black and white for impact to force a premise down your throat. Success can indeed be accompanied by feelings—pride, happiness, power, horniness, insecurity, fear, worry.

And to be sure happiness and love can also be defined with tangibles—a twenty-room mansion that makes you happy or riding around in your new Aston Martin Vanquish convertible with the top down on a sunny day, or a Bali vacation in a beachfront villa (if they even have villas in Bali... I think they do... Hmm. You know who would know? The innernet).

But lying on a public beach, bathing in the warm sun while the waves deliver a cool sea breeze over your body can make you feel happy, too. Surely time spent with your family and friends offers feelings of happiness (or... maybe it doesn't. I don't know your life... maybe time spent *away from* your family and friends makes you happy. I don't judge).

Love, too, can be described in tangible terms, like being with that one special person you've coveted from afar and finally tricked into being with you because of your new Aston Martin Vanquish convertible.

But you can also have *feelings* of love for your significant other, your children, your parents, your friends, and even your pet—I know I do. I loved my little cat William, aka Billy, aka Chilly Billy, aka Chill Bill. Spending time with him always made me happy.

It's important to note, that even when describing things like this for happiness and love, ultimately, they produce a feeling. That's why it's imperative we define all three—happiness, love, *and* success—in terms of how they make us *feel*.

Oh, and I checked with the innernet and it told me there are indeed villas in Bali. *The innernet knows all.*

Feeling Is Believing

The happiness, success, and love to which I refer are *emotions*, rather than *things*. And the way you experience them is through *feelings*. At the end of the day, no matter what you accomplish, real and true satisfaction won't come from seeing checkmarks next to completed items on a list of goals. It will come only from *feeling* it.

This is why people go to work every day and successfully accomplish the tasks mandated by their job but don't think they're successful. It's also the reason those who have achieved their dreams to become what so many others only dream of becoming—star athletes, A-list actors, idolized rock stars, powerful politicians, accomplished authors—walk away from it all. Or worse, literally destroy themselves because of it with drugs, alcohol, sex, food, or (if you can believe this) *working harder!*

When we see someone with everything they could possibly have it's normal to wonder *how could they* NOT *be happy? How could they* NOT *think they're successful? How could they just flush it all down the toilet?* (Hint: It's not what they are or do, it's how they *feel* when being and doing it.) (Actually, that wasn't really a hint—I pretty much just out and out gave you the answer.)

. . .

Putting It All Together

Here's where reading this entire goddamn book finally pays off—it's why this section of the book is titled *Putting It All Together*.

To keep on track, on point, and on time, you're going to incorporate everything we've discussed thus far when designing your new bulletproof definitions of happiness, success, and love. If you think you need a little more assistance (because you forgot everything you've already read or you never actually read it and just jumped straight to the part titled "Putting It All Together" to spare yourself all that reading), I've created an EZ-to-use cheat sheet—a collection of the top principles from this book.

EZ-TO-USE CHEAT SHEET FOR DESIGNING HAPPY, SUCCESSFUL, AND LOVING DEFINITIONS FOR HAPPINESS, SUCCESS, AND LOVE

Just Don't Try So Hard

Chant this as your mantra when developing your new definitions: *Don't try so hard... Don't try so hard... Don't try so hard.* Trying too hard is a waste of time and energy. Capitulate to the futility of effort and all its foils: the law of diminishing returns, the role of luck in achievement, and your own limitations.

Drive Your Own Car

Driving someone else's car with *their* seat positioning, mirror adjustment, and smell can be unfamiliar, difficult, even dangerous. That's why it's imperative you modify their preferences for yours: reposition that seat, adjust that mirror, and the smell... I dunno. I have no idea how to fix that. (A car detailer?) Just because you inherited someone else's predilections doesn't mean you have to keep them.

. . .

Make It a Rule ~~Not~~ to Value Your Beliefs

You've come a long way from chapter 7. Your new set of rules, values, and beliefs will be your life compass. Use them whenever you lose your way and need direction.

When Life Gives You Lemons, Make Whiskey Sours

Many of the obstacles you must avoid for happiness, success, and love are spurious snares left for you by others to protect their agendas which include guiding and controlling you for their benefit. Governments, religions, employers, and families, I'm talking to YOU. While designing your new definitions should you encounter any no-win scenarios (*contradictions, improbabilities, impossibilities*) Kobayashi Maru that shit just like Captain Kirk and Rocky did.

Embrace Mediocrity

Mediocre is the new normal. Actually, it's always been the normal, we just never wanted to admit it. But these facts exemplifying mediocrity in the pursuit of happiness, success, and love are irrefutable:

- Only a minuscule 1.1 percent of the world's population are millionaires.[2]
- Only 31 percent of American adults say they're very happy.[3]
- The divorce rate in the United States is between 40 percent and 50 percent (with 60 percent for second marriages and a whopping 73 percent of third marriages ending in divorce).[4]

Boy, with stats like those you're best off lowering the bar, aiming for the middle, and living a life of good enough.

. . .

The Three or Four No-Longer Destructive Beliefs

The constructive versions of the industrial self-help complex's "destructive beliefs."

1. Don't pressure yourself into trying harder by thinking you're better than you actually are.
2. Stephen Stills nailed it in his anthem to mediocre love: "… if you can't be with the one you love, honey, Love the one you're with." (Seriously, read that song's lyrics —they're a goddamn master class in lowering the love bar to be happy.)
3. Trust no living man, walk carefully around the dead ones. (My grandmother's immortal signature exhortation.)

Precise Ambiguity

Give your definitions some elbow room. So-called "experts" in the manifesting movement will falsely tell you the opposite is true. It isn't. They'll tell you specificity and clarity put you on a direct course with success(!). Nothing could be further from the truth or farther off course, of course. Pesky particulars are just more obstacles in the way to attainment. Within ambiguity, there is room to paralogize, compromise, and sanitize—all in *your* favor. As I've repeated over and over and over again, *specificity is the killer of dreams.*

Self-Love

It's the glue that bonds this all together. It brings authenticity to your life. Operating from the vantage point of self-love, your vision is unobstructed. You see your value and worthiness and that you truly deserve to be successful enough, happy enough, and loving enough.

. . .

Emotion > Feeling > Definition

As you design your new definitions, don't think of happiness, success, and love in terms of goals or deliverables but rather the feelings and emotions they instill in you. Create an emotion associated with each that enables you to *feel* successful, *feel* happy, and *feel* loved/in love, then design your new definitions from that state. An emotional foundation will add resonance to your definitions far beyond anything that mere status and accumulation will.

WARNING! EFFORT ALERT!
The following section involves thinking and writing. A modicum of time and effort on the part of you, the reader, will be required.

To ensure maximum benefit with minimal effort, please remember to follow these three rules:

1. Use a *single* piece of paper for the lessercise—more pages = more work.
2. Do *not* use a computer for the lessercises—embrace the *Three Ps*: paper, pencil, pen.
3. Do *not* overthink the lessercises—overthinking is overrated.

Okay, time to get out your GRID from *Step 1: Define Your Happiness, Success, and Love.* In the second, "New," column you are going to write your newly designed definitions of *happiness, success,* and *love.*

To assist you in designing your new definitions of happiness, success, and love, here's my redefining thought process for your reference...

. . .

Happiness

My first definition of happiness was a *pet giraffe*. Owing to the myriad reasons that keeping a living, full-grown giraffe penned up on my small patio is an act of insanity (and will *definitely* get me fined by my HOA), I have eliminated the impossibility not by eliminating the *giraffe*, but by changing its *location* and instead **adopting a giraffe**. It's a perfect example of the redefining process. Of course, I realize I can't have a pet giraffe, I'm not insane—one would never fit on my patio. However, there are numerous organizations that offer giraffe "adoption" packages. For a very reasonable fee (faaaaaar less than buying tons of giraffe food and paying 1-800-GOT-JUNK to haul away bulk loads of hot, steamy, wet giraffe shit) I am now the proud sponsor of a real giraffe named Kiki in Uganda. And in the process, I received:

- a personalized adoption certificate
- a beautiful fine art photo of my adopted giraffe
- my and my new giraffe's names on the Conservation Supporter Wall
- a giraffe t-shirt
- and best of all, a **plush toy giraffe** that doesn't eat or shit and that I can keep in my townhouse

I get to make a difference in the lives of those extraordinary animals of Uganda's savanna. And they benefit from the resulting conservation efforts of giraffes and their habitats. Everybody wins.

BONUS, I've also boosted my happiness quotient because now I won't have to shovel giraffe shit off my patio every day.

Next, I had a *contradiction* between **revenge on my enemies** and **being of service**. As I stated in step 2, while hellbent on seeking revenge, I cannot be of service to my enemies. Conversely, I assume being of service to others precludes plotting cold revenge against them. So, these two canceled each other out.

Since my newly minted values hold that I will experience more happiness enriching people's lives rather than destroying them (mind you, a theory I'm still not fully convinced is true, but time will tell) I combined those two contradictions into one new definition based in my new rules, values, and beliefs: **being of service to everyone**—and in some cases, that might even include my enemies. Sure, I'm taking the high road, but it's necessary for spiritual growth and happiness, so what the fuck?

Combining **revenge on my enemies** and **being of service** left me one *happiness* definition short so I added a new one: **Stargazing**. This is just what it says it is: gazing at the stars. Specifically, for me, it's looking up at the stars at night, outside, with or without a telescope.

When I was a kid back in the 1970s, I loved looking at the night sky. It made me happy. Sometimes I'd kneel on my bed, my forearms resting on my bedroom windowsill, and stare at the moon before I went to sleep. In the summer months, I'd lay on the grass in our front yard all night and look at the stars, learning and identifying dozens of constellations. On especially lucky nights I'd manage to spot a shooting star or two streaking through the suburban sky.

For Christmas 1975 I got a nifty reflector telescope, I spent hours looking at the moon, marveling at the craters and mountains in even greater detail.* My most exciting astronomical delight was when Saturn was closest to the Earth. I could actually see the rings! Forty-five years later, I still fondly recall my

---

* Oddly enough, I never saw anything ostensibly left there from our alleged "moon landings." No flags, no golf clubs, no tools. None of the cameras, ninety-six bags of human waste, or, oh, I dunno, maybe the *six* goddamn lunar modules. How about the *three* moon cars the size of Ford Pintos that're supposedly parked there like it's a lunar used car lot? Not a goddamn thing. Yeah, we went to the moon.

adventures in space even if we never really did land on the moon.

Now, I can assure you all those heartwarming tales from my idyllic childhood are embellished. I highly doubt I spent *hours* looking at the stars—I didn't have the attention span back then to finish an entire episode of the *Planet of the Apes* TV show let alone look at static shots of moon craters. My bed wasn't next to my window, it was across the room. We didn't have a lawn, instead, we had rocks and shrubs (my dad knew he'd never get my lazy ass to mow a lawn), so I'd lay on the cold, hard, concrete driveway. The only constellation I could ever make out was the "Big Dripper," as I so authoritatively called it (or was it the Little Dripper...?) And while I did see the rings around Saturn, it was actually years later at my friend's house using his more powerful telescope.

However, the important point here is that these childhood activities still make me happy. And with such simple pleasures as stargazing or flying a kite or soaking up the warm sun in a cool beach breeze so readily (and cheaply) available, happiness is always easily attainable.

Success

Starting with my first requirement, **be a rich and famous author**... As you may recall, I determined this one to be an *improbability*. But, by crossing out ~~rich~~ and ~~famous~~ and leaving *author*, I easily made this item achievable (I don't have to *beat* the champ, just *go the distance*).

As I mentioned, there are so few famous authors, and with only 1.1 percent of the world's population being millionaires why should I hang my success on two such long shots? I can still pursue fame and millions of dollars, *just not as a defining requirement for my success*.

Next, I classified **sex with a supermodel** as a pipe dream, firmly planted in the *impossibility* category (no doy). Since the whole "supermodel" aspect is what made it impossible, I simply deleted it and changed the definition to *sex with* — **anyone**. Without the supermodel component, this is now arguably only in the *improbable* category. But at least I got it out of the realm of *impossibility*.

Finally, **make people do my bidding.** Here I had a *contradiction*. Between their agendas and actions, it's really difficult to count on other people for anything. So rather than set myself up for failure by hoping against hope that people will do what I want/tell them to, I simply took the uncontrollable variable out (other people) and put in the one constant for success that I *can* count on: *me*. Now, I'll **make myself do my own bidding.**

Love

My first condition was **marriage**. The problem here is marriage involves *two* people bonded together through free will and I was only *one* of those two. That allows me only 50 percent control over my love life. For that reason, I labeled this one as a *contradiction*.

For my new definition, I stripped away all the stipulations I placed on "marriage," nonviable things like that "as long as we both shall live" pressure. Shit man, I won't hold *myself* to anything for as long as I shall live—and that's *me* not committing to *myself*. What the fuck was I thinking holding my ex to it? I also gave up my unhealthy concern of how *not* being married looks to those who expect, encourage, and even reward marriage. Thank God for the fifty percent divorce rate—it really helps level the playing field (like that generous handicap I enjoyed in my childhood bowling league).

Finally, I dropped my reverence for marriage, the magnitude of which only amplified my feelings of failure and shame over my divorce to such a deafening volume that I couldn't hear me forgive myself. Defining marriage without all those pressures and preconceptions (most of which were my own), I was left with a more simple, *loving relationship*—without labels, descriptors, or institutional demands. Just love someone and have them love me—as long as they will, or can.

Next is *my own family*. My mother, father, and grandparents have all passed away. My dad was an only child, my mom had one brother (from whom I am estranged). I have two brothers, we're close emotionally, but distant geographically. So, as far as immediate family goes, it's slim pickin's.

As I wrap up my fifth decade on earth, unmarried and not wanting to be three-quarters of a century old when my child graduates high school, having my own family falls into the *contradiction*, *improbability*, and *impossibility* categories.

The fix? If I can't broaden my family, widen my definition of it.

I met my best friend when we were *four years old*. We grew up in the same cul-de-sac together. As kids, we went to the same schools, spent holidays together, worked our first jobs together, and saw the first three *Star Wars* movies together.

As young adults, we went to college together, dormed together, were roommates after college, shared more holidays, and saw the *Star Wars* prequel movies together.

As adults, we were best man (mans? men?) at each other's weddings, spent more holidays together, shared the births of his children along with my divorce, and saw the three *Star Wars* sequels together (with *his* kids). We talk/text weekly and get together fairly regularly despite the miles between us. He's not just a friend, he's my brother. So he easily counts as *family*.

I have four other friends I've known for between forty-five and twenty-one years all of whom I consider family. We too have been through life's greatest milestones together: school, marriages, births, divorces, deaths, and *Star Wars* movies. So, I took stock of these important people in my life and realized I have a *family of friends*.

That leaves *the adoration of others*. Given all its problems (*Contradiction, Improbability, Impossibility*), this was the easiest of my definitions to redefine. I already had the solution right there in chapters 9 and 10.

Rather than needing other people to adore me, I only need the love of one person: *me*. My third and final requirement in my new definition of **Love** then is to *love myself*.

Now that we've gone through my redefining process, let's compare my original, failure-centric definitions of happiness, success, and love with my newly minted guaranteed-to-be-successful-happy-and-loved ones.

Happiness

1. *A pet giraffe* **becomes** *adopt a giraffe.*
2. *Revenge on my enemies* **becomes** *be of service to everyone —possibly even my enemies.*
3. *Being of service* **becomes** *stargazing.*

Success

1. *Be a rich and famous author* **becomes** *be an author.*
2. *Sex with a supermodel* **becomes** *sex with anyone.*
3. *Make people do my bidding* **becomes** *do my own bidding.*

Love

1. *Marriage* **becomes** *a loving relationship.*
2. *My own family* **becomes** *a family of friends.*
3. *The adoration of others* **becomes** *love myself.*

With these new definitions now included, my final GRID

(figure 18.1) becomes the physical blueprint for my happy, successful, and loving life.

Figure 18.1

I made several copies of both my GRID and *Rules, Values, and Beliefs List* and posted them in my home, workplace, and car, with smaller versions for my wallet, a PDF for my computer, and wallpaper for my phone. Everywhere I go, everyplace I look, I see my new definitions along with the rules, values, and beliefs that support them so I'm constantly reminded of my EZ pathway to happiness, success, and love through the unbridled power of mediocrity. And when you finish your GRID I encourage you to do the same.

At This Point, You're Probably Thinking…

That's it??? Adopting a giraffe?! Having sex with anyone?!?! Loving yourself?!?!?! Dude, you're really lowering the bar, aiming for the middle, and shooting straight into mediocrity. First off, thank you. Next off, since you were promised a book about happiness, success, and love, so you may also be thinking *where's the million dollars? A new big house? A fancy car? Where's my family? My significant other to grow old with? And why'd you give up on dating that supermodel?*

Well, they're all still out there for the taking. However, this book is about achieving happiness, success, and love—not scoring cash, cars, and dating supermodels (which, by the way, would be a pretty fan-fucking-tastic book, but one I have no business writing). But beware: as I've overstated countless times in this book, merely echoing the wisdom of so many others who came before me, those things can vanish faster than they appear at the drop of someone else's hat. Take it from me: aim for the middle, don't let your reach exceed your grasp, and love the one you're with.

Now It's Your Turn to Revolutionize *Your* Life

You have all the knowledge, expertise, and mediocrity I have to offer. Now it's [finally] time for you to get cracking on *your* nine NEW definitions that will guarantee you happiness, success, and love in life.

But before you go, a half-time pep talk...

During the redefining process, it's common to get stuck or feel lost. You still have decades of false hopes and hidden agendas rolling around in your brain. You'll hear them talk to you. They'll whisper all sorts of lies in your ear in an effort to derail you...

You can do better... Don't sell yourself short... What makes this Jackson guy such an expert? He's got a useless MFA for Chrissakes—that's like a six-year degree in arts and crafts.

Your mind will bargain with you. Cajole you. And shame you. It will tell you any cock and bull story to steer you away from mediocrity. RESIST THIS! DO NOT BELIEVE IT! (Well, except maybe for the part about my MFA—it is pretty useless.)

It's time to tackle your new definitions and create a life of happiness, success, and love!

You can do this! (Hell, I did.)

I'll be kicking back in the next chapter, waiting for you to finish…

CHAPTER 19

CONGRATULATIONS!

You can't have everything. Where would you put it?
—Steven Wright

If you've previously had nothing, then you have plenty of room to put everything.
—M.K. Jackson

You're reading this so that can only mean one thing: **Congratulations, you did it!** You have bravely weathered the time and effort necessary to triumphantly complete your new and *greatly improved* definitions of *happiness*, *success*, and *love* based on *your* (new) rules, values, and beliefs, and rooted in the fundamentals of mediocrity. This calls for a celebration!

BONUS: Pomp and Circumstance

Just because this book is neither formidable nor an achievement is no reason you shouldn't receive some form of accreditation for sticking it out. So, to make it official (and formidable and an achievement)…

As a graduate of this book, I hereby confer upon you, the degree of Master of Mediocrity—with a FREE downloadable diploma.*

To get your diploma, jump on the information superhighway and log onto:

www.aimforthemiddlebook.com/diploma

1. Download the *Master of Mediocrity* diploma.
2. Print your diploma.
3. Use fancy-pants parchment paper for that "real diploma" look.
4. Add one of those shiny gold certificate seal stickers to make it look even more "official."
5. Display your certificate of completion prominently— in your home, workplace, on social media, your dating profile, the rear car window—anywhere you want others to see and envy your mediocreic accomplishment.

---

* And yes, I am completely aware that some readers of this book may have skipped over the entire text, gone straight to this section, saw the free diploma offer, downloaded it, and are currently displaying a Master of Mediocrity degree without actually doing any of the work to earn it. I'm also aware that makes them summa cum laude graduates; those of the highest distinction. I mean anyone who does that has truly mastered the whole concept of this book—and without even reading it. *That's* impressive and totally deserves a gold seal.

. . .

Now What?

Now you apply your new definitions to your everyday life pursuits from now on for as long as you live, that's what now what.

Because *you* designed them for *yourself*, implementing them in your life will be second nature (actually, I guess it would be more like *first* nature). And once you do, you'll be happy, successful, and loving for the rest of your life. Wow!

But Wait, There's Even More! *The Five Pillars of an Adequate Life*

As a double-added extra bonus, the following (and, thank God, final) part of this book, titled "The Five Pillars of an Adequate Life," is a handy-dandy, how-to supplement to assist you in achieving happiness, success, and love with concepts and strategies including lowering your expectations, embracing complacency, and taking a SHIT every day.

It probably seems like more work, but really it's akin to the CliffsNotes for this book; an easy shortcut on the pathway to happiness, success, and love through the unbridled power of mediocrity—and at no extra charge to you!

Virtus mediocritatis excedit scientiam!

PART THREE
THE FIVE PILLARS OF AN ADEQUATE LIFE

PILLAR ONE: LOWER YOUR EXPECTATIONS

The secret to happiness is having low expectations.
—Warren Buffett

And that's coming from a guy who has, like, a bajillion dollars—so you know I'm right.
—M. K. Jackson

The first key to an adequate life is *lowering your expectations*. On everything. Nothing throws a wrench into happiness, success, and yes, even love, faster, harder, and with greater accuracy than expecting more from yourself and others.

That wide, deep chasm between what you *expect* of something or someone (including yourself) and what is actually delivered is where disappointment, heartache, and unhappiness reside rent-free. You cannot fill that abyss with patience, positive thinking, or even threats. Into its depths you must lower your expectations—it's the only way out.

In 1984 I bought tickets for the opening-day screening of *Indiana Jones and the Temple of Doom*. Having seen and loved *Raiders of the Lost Ark*, I couldn't wait for the sequel. This *Temple of Doom* flick was from the two guys who not only made *Raiders*, but *Jaws, Star Wars, Close Encounters of the Third Kind,* and *The Empire Strikes Back.* These guys knew what they were doing. You could bet the temple on it.

My girlfriend and I went opening day with advanced tickets (and this was back in the day, before the innernet. You had to stand in line for hours, even days for pre-sale tix.) We arrived several hours early for choice seats (this was back in the day before assigned seating and you had to queue your ass for hours or even days for a good seat). The time we spent getting the tickets and then waiting to get in the theatre was longer than the running time of the movie. But we knew it would all be worth it.

We eagerly settled into our seats. The lights went down! The screen lit up! And the three-year wait was finally over!!!

The first shot: the Paramount Pictures logo match dissolving into a mountain on a giant gong. YES! Clever! Just like in *Raiders.* This is gonna be great!

But then, not thirty seconds into the movie, something felt... off.

An opening dance number? WTF? *Hmmm... Okay, maybe... Let's see where this goes...* Then the Busby Berkeley boner became a bonkers balloon-bursting boogie for a poison antidote. WTFF? Sure, running behind the giant rolling gong for protection from the gunfire was cool—but completely inaccurate.* Little did I know at the time, this would seem like a scientific metallurgy documentary compared to what awaited us.

We were now ten minutes in, and this didn't feel like an Indiana Jones movie—more like a James Bond film—one of the Roger Moore ones. Things then moved from silly to goofy when Indy jumped out the window of the Club *Obi Wan* (WTFFF?)

---

* Anything less than two inches of solid steel (which a gong usually is), and the bullets would go right through it. However, taking into account the forensic evidence we have of the "magic bullet" from the Kennedy assassination, anything is possible when bullets start flying around. So, I suspended my disbelief on this one. However, I had NO IDEA as to the degree of testing to my suspending that awaited me in this movie.

with the screaming torch singer because she had the antidote he needed stashed in her bra (WTFFFF?) Easier to take her along than feel her up, I figured (good to know Indy's a gentleman, even when dying of poisoning). When the two landed in the getaway car it's revealed that Indy's partner on this adventure, the person he will rely on to fill the gaps in his knowledge and abilities (as he did with the knowledgeable and capable Sallah in *Raiders*) would be a ten-year-old boy. WTFFFFF?

This was too much to swallow even for a porn star. Our heroes jumped out of a plane in a rubber life raft and lived to tell about it. Weak, malnourished, children enslaved by the evil cult for heavy manual labor. Indy in a trance. And just for the hell of it, a *Three's Company* boob joke. WTFFFFFF, F, F, and F?

As I retraced my steps, attempting to discover the exact point where this whole thing went off the rails, it *literally* went off the rails in a mining car chase when the cart jumped off, then successfully landed back on, the track. WTFFFFFFFFFF???

And just when it seemed like it couldn't get any worse, it did. With our heroes trapped in the middle of a rickety rope bridge high above an alligator-infested riverbed, Indy chopped the bridge in two. As they all held on, their half of the bridge smashed into the side of a rocky cliff—*and everyone survived.* WTFFFFFFFFFFF? I waited three fucking years for a Wile E. Coyote cartoon? What was next? An Acme anvil dropping on Indy's head? *Raiders* surely had its own fantastic elements, but it always maintained verisimilitude by never breaking logic within the *natural* universe and by separating it from the *supernatural* universe. Crawling under a moving truck? Sure. Human bodies smashing into a jagged cliffside and surviving? C'mon.

When the movie finally, mercifully ended and the lights came up, my girlfriend and I looked at one another with an unspoken acknowledgment between two people who had just been fleeced by the same conman's scam but were too ashamed to admit it. WTFFFFFFFFFFFF?!

I had to check the credits to see if this was one of those

crappy switcheroo sequels made by different people who suck, like *Airplane II*, *Caddyshack II*, or *Staying Alive*. But nope, these were indeed the same folks who made *Raiders*. I mean, I wasn't expecting *The Godfather, Part II*, but what in the Sam Hill went wrong? They *owed* me a great sequel like *The Empire Strikes Back* and they reneged!

I was able to diffuse the trauma by becoming embittered. The bitterness eventually turned to regret, which finally became apathy (the *Three Stages of Cinematic Grief*). I was hit with the reality that even those whom I elevated into the stratosphere of creative infallibility had feet of Play-Doh.

As I continued to talk myself off the ledge of letdown, it dawned on me that not only were these the *Jaws/Star Wars/Close Encounters/Empire/Raiders* guys, they were also *The Star Wars Holiday Special/Twilight Zone: The Movie/More American Graffiti/1941* guys. George and Steve were just two guys making a movie. *I* was the one who made *Temple of Doom* into more than it was and less than they delivered.

I took an important lesson away from that traumatic cinematic event: to be truly happy—in *anything*—**the most I should expect from others is the least I would expect from myself.** I know, I know: easier said than done. We all find ourselves expecting more from everyone (including ourselves). We do it because we're looking for others to fulfill our happiness, success, and love. It's reckless and dangerous. And I promise you (well, *promise* is probably a little too emphatic)… I can *tell* you the only real, true way to be happy, successful, and loving is to *lower all expectations*. But how do we do that? Well, it's really rather simple…

Learn to LYE

Interviewing for that dream job you know you'll never get but really want? *LYE.*

Forced to spend the holidays with your family but want to enjoy yourself anyway? Just *LYE*.

Want a happy, harmonious relationship with the love of your life? You're *definitely* gonna have to *LYE*.

LYE is **Lower Your Expectations**.

Because expectations are a surefire way to experience all the disappointment we cannot handle, if you desire any semblance of happiness, success, and/or love in your life, LYEing is something you better start doing yesterday.

I had no control over *Indiana Jones and the Temple of Doom*—if I did, I would have cut that ridiculous bridge sequence. But since I can't raise the bridge, I'll lower my expectations. And now I can accept that *Temple of Doom* is not the great movie I wanted it to be, but rather the mediocre movie it actually is. And you know what? *Mediocre is more than adequate.*

Of the first four films in the Indiana Jones franchise, *Temple of Doom* has the third lowest aggregated critical rating,[1] third lowest audience rating, and has made the least amount of money. Even Steven Spielberg, the guy who directed the goddamn movie says *Temple of Doom* is *his* least favorite Indiana Jones film.[2]

Yet despite all that, the flick has a lifetime gross of $333,107,271, (from just a $28,000,000 budget)[3] and a rabid fanbase who express the delusional belief that *Temple of Doom* is the best of the Indiana Jones films. Certainly not bad achievements for a mediocre movie. *Mediocre is more than adequate.*

So how, then, do we lower our expectations? Fortunately, LYEing is a lot easier than you might think—especially when using a simple formula I've created for getting those expectations down where they belong...

The Sixty Percent Reduction Rule

This rule states that in all aspects of your life, from the most minor to the most major, every single one of your expectations is perilously too high and must be beaten down into submission. Otherwise, it's gonna backfire in your face...

- Expecting to finally get your first raise after twenty years on the job? *It's gonna backfire in your face.*
- Expecting you won't be laid off from your job because you *didn't* get a raise? *It's gonna backfire in your face.*
- Expecting your significant other won't cheat on you? *It's gonna backfire in your face.*
- Expecting your children will graduate high school? *It's gonna backfire in your face.*
- Expecting the drive-through burger joint will get your order correct? *It's gonna backfire in your face.*
- Expecting your car to start when you turn the key? *It's gonna backfire in your face.*

In fact, the only thing that won't backfire in your face is that *everything's gonna backfire in your face.* And that's what the *Sixty Percent Rule* remedies. It's an anti-backfiring-in-you-face method for setting more realistic expectations that will not leave you feeling like a miserable, lonely failure. Here's how it works: simply reduce everything you've dreamed about, had your heart set on, worked for, or thought you deserved by *sixty percent.*

For example, if you thought there was a ninety percent chance you were going to have a life full of love, adventure, and meaning, reduce that by sixty percent. Now there's only a *thirty percent chance* of that happening and *now* you're being realistic. With only a mere thirty percent you will no longer be invested in the outcome—and you won't be disappointed when it doesn't happen. So, if by some chance there's another Miracle of the Sun and Our Lady of Fatima hands over a *fifth* secret that—*behold!*—you ARE gonna have a life full of love, adventure, and meaning, well, then bonus!

What's great about the *Sixty Percent Reduction Rule* is it works for *everything* in your life no matter how major or minor.

Think there's a 100 percent chance you're having chicken for dinner tonight? Lower that expectation by sixty percent, now there's only a *forty percent chance* of you having chicken. Now when you arrive at the supermarket to an empty chicken section and some putz beats you to the last box of frozen Banquet fried chicken, you are totally sympatico with Hamburger Helper for dinner.

But the true genius of the *Sixty Percent Reduction Rule* is when applying it lowers the expectation percentage into the *negative* range. Don't worry when this happens—it's a good thing. In fact, the *Sixty Percent Reduction Rule* is designed to render negative possibility percentages to really tamp down all hope of something happening. That way, you're not left holding a bag of broken dreams. Actually, it's more like a bag filled with previously expected but never happens.

For example: if the expectation that you will someday have love in your life is (an overly optimistic) thirty percent—no, wait, make that a more realistic twenty-five percent—reducing it by sixty percent means you now have a *negative thirty-five* percent chance of it ever happening. *Negative thirty-five percent!* Boy, there's *no way* you can ever expect it to happen now. So, if it never happens, you'll be far less devastated. BUT, if it *does* happen just think of how much more unexpected and exciting it will be. Win-win! It's like a girlfriend of mine used to tell me:

"If you don't expect it, you won't be disappointed when it doesn't happen."

Wise words to live (and love) by.

LYEing by Omission

Another method to insulate yourself from the disappointment of other people's underdelivering is to simply cut everyone out of your life. And thanks to all the amazing anti-social advancements made during the Great Pandemic of 2020, it's never been easier to do.

You can get a job working remotely and avoid in-person contact with over-motivated bosses, supervisors, and coworkers who incessantly push you to do better by using words like "focus," "cadence," "excellence," and of course, "team"—like you're all athletes or horses.

You can shop for a romantic partner online, have virtual dates, sexting, even cybersex! And thanks to the groundbreaking advancements made by the Japanese in sex robots, you no longer have to date real people, listen to them drone on about their lives, and pretend to care. With these robots, you can skip all that interpersonal bullshit and get to the point of getting laid. Man, I wish I was in my twenties again!

And nowadays using the internet, you can even easily fake your own death so family, friends, and loved ones will leave you alone. Seriously, Google that shit.

Unfortunately, the only person you cannot evade is yourself. To quote Buckaroo Banzai: *No matter where you go, there you are** —emphasis on *you*. Ultimately, you're the only one who can abjure the forlorn expectations of distinction that have inequitably sabotaged your happiness, success, and love. That's why LYEing to yourself is so important.

When you lower your personal expectations, you set the stage for happiness and success by *omission*. All those unattainable chimeras—the best job, the most passionate romance, making a difference—are eliminated, freeing you up to pursue more practical and securable objectives. *Give yourself a break. You don't need to work so hard when you can just be mediocre.*

Now, I understand your initial response will likely be to push back. To say: *I'm not lowering my expectations—I refuse to settle for second best!* And I agree. Never settle for second best. To be *truly* happy, successful, and in love beyond all expectations, you

---

* Actually, this aphorism is attributed to Jim Russell in the March 4, 1955, edition of the *Hazleton Collegian*, a Pennsylvania State University student publication. But Jim Russell, as witty as he may have been, was no Buckaroo Banzai.

should settle for third best—maybe even fourth or fifth best. Second best is still a little too close for comfort.

Become a Professional LYEr

LYEing in your career is better than any degree, certification, training, or nepotism (just ask a politician). Tragically, for too many of us, our professional lives become intertwangled with our personal lives. We allow our job to define us as individuals and validate our self-worth. Given the transitory nature of a job/career/occupation, no real good can ever come of this. Ever.

Consider these oft-asked questions used to define the degree of a person's professional success:

- How much money do you make?
- Is your pay at least triple your age?
- Is your job blue-collar or white-collar?
- Retail?
- Service industry?
- How much money do you make?
- Do you toil in a cubicell™ or do you have your own office?
- If you have your own office, does it have a window?
- Is your own office with a window a corner office?
- How much money do you make?
- Do you have to wear a uniform?
- Do you have to wear a nametag?
- Is your supervisor younger than you?
- How much money do you make?

All these questions are bullshit, really. Motivators of grief for something most of us don't even want to be doing. Yet, somehow, it's all become very important—to others and ourselves. So important that we concoct nonsensical goals with onerous deadlines as part of some harebrained master plan for salary bumps, corner offices, title recognition, and culture assimilation with a company we know by name yet ignore in reputation.

The last thing you should hitch your wagon to is an employer's star because, buddy, that star can burn out at any second, leaving you floating all alone in the cold, lonely vacuum of deep office space. However, since the vast majority of us must bring home the bacon, fry it up in a pan, and never let you forget you're a man,[4] LYEing is the perfect formula for happiness and then success in one's professional pursuits.

After I was unceremoniously given the heave-ho by my previous employer, I was especially heedful when setting sail for the new job world. Having navigated the severance seas before, I set these LYEing expectations for my next job:

- A paycheck
- A chair to sit in at my desk
- A bathroom on the premises

When I landed my next job, you know what I got? Everything I wanted. And let me tell you, achieving every one of my employment objectives made me feel *very* successful—and happy.

LYE in Love

When it comes to love (pursuing, being in, and the making of) the applied practice for lowering your expectations is called *punching your weight*. And since you are reading this book, there is a distinct probability that you have been told, perhaps somewhat emphatically by a well-meaning friend or even the indifferent recipient of your amorous pursuits, to execute this concept with extreme prejudice (I know I have). As difficult as it may be to swallow, this is sage advice. Best put aside the demoralizing feelings of inadequacy it engenders and embrace it as the profound teachable moment it truly is (I know I haven't).

If you think you can successfully punch above your weight you are deceiving yourself. It's your ego talking. And your ego is a cruel, heartless bastard who has no skin in the game when it comes to lovelorn humiliation. Your ego will surrender *your* best interests in favor of *its* best interest and never the twain shall meet.

Look: it's admirable (I guess) to think you're capable of ensnaring someone superior to you in every way—genetically, intellectually, financially—but it is, nevertheless, delusional. Such misguided folly is no doubt from seeing too many rom-coms in which the diffident protagonist successfully punches above their weight winning over the object of their affections after chasing them to the airport in the quixotic climax. The mismatched lovers embrace. The end. Cue peppy pop song. Roll credits. Aaaaannnnd do NOT try this bullshit in real life. It is a sadistic trope of the Hollywood Screenwriting Illuminati to instill the false hope in you that you can punch above your weight so you'll keep watching their preposterous cinematic concoctions.

Personally, I know of no universe where I hook up with Monica Bellucci. Ever. I'm sure there's a universe where I'm the old guy parking her car or the old guy wearing an ankle monitor living in a studio apartment with a shared bathroom and a hotplate with dozens of her photos taped to my walls. But *dating* her? No. No fucking way. And you know what, I'm totally a-okay with that. (Well, not the shared bathroom part. That sorta creeps me out.) I'm okay with the rest of it because I know I gotta punch my weight.

You're Never Too Young to LYE

Don't think this lowering one's expectations sensation is just for adults. LYEing is for all ages—young and old alike... *especially the young*.

Every morning when I go over my top five regrets in life,

number one with a bullet is always *not lowering my expectations when I was younger*. When we're children, life has yet to kick us in the groin so hard and so often that we can't breathe or see straight. We've yet to learn just how little we can actually achieve so we believe everything is possible. Throughout our youth, we carry this reckless sense of inflated self-potential aided and abetted by adults who really should know better.

By the time we set out in our adult life, we're like that truck in the movie *Sorcerer* packed with nitroglycerine, crossing the dilapidated rope bridge, ever so slowly, inch by inch, waiting for a slat to snap, plunging us into a combustible river-of-no-return.

If only our expectations had been tamped down when we were still young enough for it to do some real good, we could've reached our mediocre potential much earlier and with greater acceptance. Perhaps then we wouldn't have lugged all that magical thinking into adulthood where it caused real damage.

When I work with grade school and high school kids, coaching them for life, the first thing I tell them the same thing:

"Now, while you are young, is the time to lower your expectations and lay the foundation of mediocrity upon which you will one day build your adult life."

And I have to tell you, kids nowadays *get it*. They are naturally so much more mediocre than we ever were at their age. With twenty-four/seven innernet access in the palms of their sweaty little hands, not only do they embrace mediocrity, they've invented new ways to express it: Snapchatting every single quotidian aspect of their lives (food pix!), distilling written communication down to literacy-defying abbreviations and symbols (emojis!), lip-syncing to songs, lip-syncing to movie and TV dialogue, even lip-syncing to someone else's lip-synching songs, movie, and TV dialogue, they intuitively understand the whole mediocrity thing. Supported by social media and influencer role models, they collect and covet "likes" with the same life-depends-on-it zeal that I do at month's end with my blood pressure pills. And given their self-important nullification of all historical, social, and cultural events that happened before they were born, we would all do well to learn from them.

Get That Mediocrity Monkey on Your Back

The Temple of Doom case study can be applied to life as well. It's not a bad life, it's just mediocre—and that's great news! Mediocrity is *the* surefire pathway to happiness, success, and, yes, even love. With your expectations lowered, mediocrity flourishes. Most importantly (and I do mean *most*), mediocrity is something you, me, or anyone can achieve. Now, I realize that at first, the very idea of being mediocre may be difficult for you to swallow while choking on the decades of false hope you've been fed (specifically, that *you can do if you can dream it* nonsense). But it's *lowering your expectations* that will empower you to accept and embrace mediocrity—yours, as well as everyone else's. And I promise you, under mediocrity's blissful ignorance, you will be happier in every aspect of your life. The pressures to achieve beyond your abilities simply melt away, along with all the associated anxiety and self-loathing. And like the warm, glowing effects of smack, you'll become addicted to it. You'll become a *mediocrity junkie!*

PILLAR TWO: EMBRACE COMPLACINCY

There are days when I think I'm going to die of an overdose of complacency.
—Salvador Dali

The greatest gift for happiness, success, and love I ever gave to myself was to overconfidently embrace my limitations. Oh, how powerful it is when you blissfully know where your abilities end and your deficiencies begin.
—M. K. Jackson

Complacency may well be the ace in your mediocre toolbox for achieving happiness, success, and love. Yet, you wouldn't know it from the agenda-driven anti-complacency diet that's shoveled down your gullet daily by the self-help industrial complex—not to mention corporate, religious, and government stakeholders. As a result, complacency has been framed as a pestilence of biblical proportions that maliciously decimates God's laws of capitalism, the morality of the human soul, and the United States of America itself(!)

But is it true?

Much of this semantic sleight of hand is derived from the presentation of selective facts. In this case, the definition of the word *complacent*. Surf the information superhighway for rah-rah team-building companies whose business it is to assimilate employees into the corporate hive mentality and the definition you'll most often see is from the *American Heritage Dictionary*:

Satisfied with the current situation and unconcerned with changing it, often to the point of smugness.

Yikes! That *is* evil! No wonder swarm intelligence taskmasters consort with the *AHD* to keep the minions in their place. But this is NOT the *only* definition out there. Let's see what other dictionaries versed in English verse have to say…

Merriam-Webster Dictionary:
marked by self-satisfaction especially when accompanied by unawareness of actual dangers or deficiencies.
Hmmm… nothing wrong with satisfaction over one's undertakings—although the unawareness of deficiencies *might* be a concern (then again, that depends on *who* is defining what a "deficiency" is).

The *Oxford Learner's Dictionaries*:
too satisfied with yourself or with a situation, so that you do not feel that any change is necessary:
Not bad at all. Confidence in a job well done, no second guessing yourself. I'll take that.

The *Cambridge Dictionary*:
feeling so satisfied with your own abilities or situation that you feel you do not need to try any harder:
Yahtzee! *That's* the definition that works best for *me*—and it's the official *complacency* meaning for *this* book.

The point I'm making with this game of dictionary diversion is they've got their definitions, I've got mine—and we'll each employ the one that best substantiates our conclusions. We *should* rest on our laurels. It's a *good* thing when we're feeling so satisfied with our abilities or a situation that we feel we don't need to try any harder.

Take me for example. I know I misspelled *complacency* in the chapter title but I'm so complacent, I don't give a fuck. I am so beyond sure that this book will still be just as good or just as bad regardless of whether I misspelled a word that I'm just gonna leave it as-is and go to press. *That's* how complacent *I* am.

I realize my abilities are mediocre. I know I'm far less likely to cure cancer than I am to cure a ham, and I'm at total peace with that because there is no greater impediment to a happy, successful, love-filled life than ambition. So many of us work so hard despite our actual abilities. We refuse to accept what little we are truly capable of and instead strive for a "level of excellence" carelessly applied across the board for all people by some self-improvement guru peddling their book, podcast, newsletter, social media, video, seminar, webinar, bloginar, vloginar, teleinar or some other inane "inar." *

Complacency: The Ultimate Success Formula

Because complacency celebrates our innate mediocrity (without apologies) it receives a bad rap from the self-help industrial complex—a wrong I would *love* to right if I just weren't so complacent.

When practiced correctly and successfully, complacency is a Zen state of being; a "feeling of calm satisfaction"—which is the best feeling to have.[1] It's expecting less from yourself while knowing better than to expect more. It is neither smug nor arro-

---

* And by the way, I have HAD IT with this crackbrained practice of adding "inar" after any communication platform when using it to present a seminar. Do you know what a seminar on the web is? IT'S A SEMINAR! You know what a seminar held in a hotel conference room is? A hotelinar? NO! IT'S A GODDAMN SEMINAR! If I show you photos on the web they're not webotos, they're FUCKING PHOTOS! Just like a seminar on the web is a FUCKING SEMINAR!!! (Besides, who even uses the word "web" for the innernet anymore? *The 90s called: AOL wants its world wide web dialup back.*)

gant, merely an expression of confident achievement when you know deep inside you have reached the zenith of your commitment, ability, and awareness. Simply stated, complacency is knowing better than to try harder while being confident enough not to care.

So, here then is my simple, EZ, **Two-step Complacency Formula** for a life of success, happiness, and love...

STEP ONE: Establish and accept *your* definitions of happiness, success, and love as the *single source of truth.*

This is pretty much what this entire goddamn book is about. Forgo, forswear, forbid, renounce, reject, and repudiate those previous agenda-driven definitions from partisan institutions that were an anchor around your neck. Consider them as irrelevant as Tom Selleck's mustache.*

Now that you've eighty-sixed those rancid old rules, values, and beliefs to create your very own brand spankin' new definitions of happiness, success, and love, OWN THEM! From now on, they are the ONLY metric by which you will ascertain whether you are successful, happy, and loving. They are now your *single source of truth.*

STEP TWO: Deploy complacency in tandem with your definitions of being happy, successful, and loving.

You already did the hard work of defining what makes YOU happy, successful, and loving. Step two is allowing complacency to wash over you like a warm ocean wave. Or a gentle summer

---

* Granted, Tom Selleck's mustache was once a success that many people loved and were happy to see. But that was then, before Tom was selling reverse mortgages and allegedly taking 1.4 million gallons of water from a fire hydrant and delivering it to his estate's avocado farm—even though he doesn't even like avocados (he says they make him gag). WTFT?

breeze cooling you from the heat of the radiant sun. Or a hot shower after sweaty prostahoe sex.

Whichever way, complacency is the succor to feeling completely satisfied with yourself and your abilities regardless of what anyone else thinks. When you're complacent, you're *sure* of it... even to the point of smugness.

PILLAR THREE: FOR GOD'S SAKE, STOP SETTING GOALS

A goal is a dream with a deadline.
—Napoleon Hill

I have enough deadlines in my waking life. I don't need them in my dreams, too.
—M.K. Jackson

I have a business proposition for you. It's an investment opportunity. You give me $20,000, and in one week, I promise you an eight percent chance to double your money—with a ninety-two percent chance you'll lose it all. Interested? If you are, then I suggest you continue setting goals, because according to a study by the University of Scranton, ninety-two percent of people who set goals never actually achieve them, leaving a measly eight percent who do.[1]

But how can it be that what the self-help industrial complex touts as the best way to become the best *you* you can become has such a lousy rate of return? Some of the more common reasons are:

- lack of strong commitment to the goals
- the goals themselves are not motivating

- too many goals
- fear of failure
- fear of success
- becoming distracted
- giving up
- too tired
- the dog ate the goals
- life in the fast lane

Eighty percent of us never even bother to set goals for ourselves so kudos, I guess, to the remaining twenty percent who at least gave it a shot, right? Well, not really. What the self-help industrial complex doesn't want you to know is of that twenty percent who do set goals, a whopping seventy percent fail to achieve the goals they set. Now, I'm not good enough at statistical math to come up with some catchy percentage-based ratio to illustrate the odds against achieving goals using some everyday triviality—like, say, the difficulty of solving a Rubik's Cube... or actually getting through that second *Avatar* movie (three hours... really?)... or even getting through that first *Avatar* movie—but I can tell you this: the odds are pretty astronomical.

But if that seventy of the twenty of the eighty percent failing is not enough to convince you of the foolhardiness of goal setting, here are five pitfalls to achieving your goals that hopefully will...

1. Goals have a negative effect on you.

At the end of the day, the only thing goal setting really does is make you feel bad about yourself for *not* achieving them. As we've established, statistically the odds of you achieving your goals are so astronomical you're setting yourself up for certain failure (which is the very opposite of success. Really, look it up).

· · ·

2. You have to write them down.

It's one thing to fail quietly, but it's an entirely different thing to keep a written record of your failure for posterity—especially in a "loser journal." I mean, what kind of a masochist are you? For the love of God, don't leave a paper trail of your inadequacy.

3. Goals are simply too much damn work.

Top goal-setting "experts" agree that accomplishing goals is a multi-level, arduous process. You have to brainstorm your goals, write them down, design a step-by-step pathway to each goal, write the pathways down, set a deadline for each goal, set a deadline for each pathway, make all your goals trackable, visualize your success, make a commitment to your goals, make a commitment to yourself, make a commitment to others (so you're "on the hook"), muster the motivation for achieving your goals, take action, hold yourself accountable, hold others accountable for holding you accountable, have your goals hold you accountable, track your progress (if any), evaluate that progress (if any), solicit feedback from others on your progress (if any), focus on positive thinking, challenge yourself to work harder and do better, reset your goals if necessary, and keep your eyes on the prize. *Whew.* That's a lot of work just so you can fail at something.

Just the sheer number of goals you have to set (never mind that insane process to accomplish them) renders goal-setting counterproductive. And stupid. Minute goals, hourly goals, daily goals, weekly goals, monthly goals, yearly goals, lifetime goals. Where does it end?! Afterlife goals? You'll have so many goddamned goals you'll never get anything done—living or dead. Seriously, *yearly* goals? I doubt I'll even be alive in a year. Why the hell should I squander my precious remaining time on earth chasing phantoms that will never materialize?

To be one of the successful eight percent from that thirty percent of those twenty percent from the initial eighty percent who never even bothered to set goals is like rolling a huge, monstrous doughnut up a hill; sure, with a lot of hard work and sweat you could probably do it, but wouldn't you rather skip the hill and just eat the doughnut?

4. Goal setting is pointless.

Once you realign your rules, values, and beliefs to support *your* vision of happiness and success, goal-setting becomes senseless. You'll have all you need to be happy and successful. Don't go mucking it all up by doing something reckless and irresponsible like creating *more* obstacles between you and your perfect life with goals.

5. Goals defeat their purpose.

So-called goals purportedly help you realize your dreams of happiness and success. Yet chasing them ironically becomes the primary impediment to the benefits they allegedly create. To better understand this paradox, here are the top six reasons "experts" claim goals are necessary along with my reasons why they're full of shit.

<u>1. "Goals give you focus."</u>

Yes, goals do give you focus—on goals. But you need to think *big picture*. With this fallacious argument, the goal itself becomes the goal, not your happiness and success.

When I was a kid, and my mom made pancakes for breakfast, she grabbed a bowl, dumped some mix in, cracked an egg, poured the milk, mixed that shit up, and dropped the batter on the griddle. Done. They were perfectly delicious hotcakes. I remember one time asking her "How do you know how much to use—don't you have to read the directions?" My mom looked at me, thoroughly offended, and socked me in the chops.

I got her point: she could've wasted all her time reading the recipe for the size of the bowl, the exact amount of mix, the precise measure of milk, the correct number of eggs, pausing each step of the way to read the instructions, wasting precious time following each step to the letter until it was dinner time. But the focus wasn't the process of flapjacks—it was getting them in our guts where they belonged.

2. "Goal setting helps you continually improve."

Does it really? If the success rate of goals is an abysmal eight percent, what are you improving? I'll tell you what: you're improving at failing. And the last time I checked a dictionary, "failure" was still an antonym for "success." In addition, how happy can you be knowing you are continually failing?

3) "Goals compel you to take action."

The only thing goals compel you to take action on is goals—as well as the long-ass laundry list of shit you gotta do to achieve those goals (see: #3 *Goals are simply too much damn work*). Seriously, with that eight percent success rate for goals, you have a better chance using creative visualization to manifest what you want. At least then you'll have envisioned the end result.

4) "Goals create a pathway to success."

Goals are not a pathway to happiness and success, they're a detour from it. As we all know by now, *mediocrity* is the pathway to happiness and success. Allow me to illustrate this immutable fact of my universe with another forced metaphorical example...

Imagine you have a medical ailment. I dunno, say it's toenail fungus. But like really *bad* toenail fungus. The kind that needs a doctor's attention. The kind where the nail's all brown, brittle, and oddly misshapen. (This actually happened to me, that's why I'm using it.) There's a doctor who is a mere three-minute walk from your house. But this doctor's Yelp rating is a mediocre two and a half stars, and you want the "best" for your contaminated, crackly claw. You find a five-star doctor waaaaaaay across town who's supposedly the "best" when it comes to treating gnarled, mildewy toes. But the soonest available appointment is in a week and you don't want that two-and-a-half star quack scraping your fetid foot, you want the best so you wait a week.

When appointment day finally arrives, you limp to the bus stop followed, by several neighborhood cats, because your moldy, ungula now smells like tuna. You'd rather drive than take the bus, but your burning fungus foot is so numb it can't operate a gas pedal. You board the bus and you're finally on your way—until the next stop. And the next. And the next. The damn bus keeps stopping at every other corner. Twenty minutes later, still stopping. Forty minutes later, a detour into a shopping center.

Finally, an hour and ten minutes later, the bus stops at the doctor's office. Well, not exactly *at* the office because the bus doesn't stop on the same block as the doctor's office. Now you have a fifteen-minute walk, dragging your throbbing, smelly, fungal-filled foot painfully behind you. But it doesn't matter because you're so late, you missed your appointment—but not as much as you're gonna miss your toe. Because you demanded the "best" doctor and waited a week instead of going with the mediocre doctor at the time, the fungus spread, you missed your appointment, and your toe fell off.

Going with the "best" may have *seemed* like the better way, but at what cost? A severed toe that looks like a mushroom? All those bus stops are like the goals on the pathway to success. They do nothing but impede you from gaining what would truly make you happy in life (like happiness, success, love, or your toe). Fact is, both doctors would've prescribed antifungal medication. Big whoop if the mediocre doctor might take a little longer or cause a few more side effects. At least you'd still have your toe.

<u>5) "Goals keep you motivated"</u>

WRONG. Happiness, success, and love keep you motivated. Goaling and doing all the subsequent work associated with goals (see: 3. *Goals are a lot of work*) keeps you exhausted. If there was any proof I could've come up with that goal setting actually worked, then I'd say, "Sure, go for it. Goal the shit out of it." But I couldn't because there isn't.

Making some progress might motivate you. But as it stands, you're best served being motivated to stop setting goals.

6) "Goals help you measure progress"

There ain't a whole lot of progress in a ninety-two percent failure rate—unless, of course, you're measuring how your frustration, shame, and sense of hopelessness are progressing. Simply stated, cut them goals loose and spend more time (re)defining happiness, success, and love within the parameters of mediocrity (as outlined in this book). It'll be so much easier—and so much more effective.

WARNING! EFFORT ALERT!
The following section involves thinking and writing. A modicum of time and effort on the part of you, the reader, will be required.

For maximum benefit with minimal effort, please remember:

1. Use a *single* piece of paper for the lessercise—more pages = more work.
2. Do *not* use a computer for the lessercises—embrace the *Three Ps*: paper, pencil, pen.
3. Do *not* overthink the lessercises—overthinking is overrated.

THE GOAL UN-SETTING WORKSHOP
Now that you understand the dangers of goal setting, there is one final step to free you from the prison of goals: *The Goal Un-Setting Workshop*. It's a very simple three-step lessercise...

1. Gather any pieces of paper upon which you have ever senselessly written any goals (from a journal,

   notebook, cocktail napkin, old restraining order,
   whatever) and place them all in a metal pan or pot.
2. Strike a match, flick a Bic, or blow a torch and set those
   goal-infested pieces of paper on fire.
3. Flush the ashes down the toilet.

That's all there is to it.

Now you can take all the time you have just saved on *not* pursuing those ineffectual goals and successfully do something you love that truly makes you happy—like napping on green grass under the warm sun, binge-watching your favorite TV shows/movies, or enjoying a delicious piece of pineapple upside-down cake.

PILLAR FOUR: CONDEMN YOUR LEGACY BUILDING

If you knew how quickly people forget the dead, you would stop living to impress people.
  —Christopher Walken

"People always forget me and I'm still alive."
  —M. K. Jackson

Y our sixth-grade report card.
  The weather report from March 26, 1994.
Your ex having sex with their new partner.
Meatballs replaced by meatcubes.

Let's see... what other inconsequential crap can you waste your time worrying about?

Oh, I know!

Your legacy.

When my grandmother died, it fell upon me to select her casket (she couldn't do it because she was dead). Browsing the showroom, I saw a split-couch model with the head section open. There, mounted permanently inside the satin-lined lid was Leonardo's *The Last Supper*. It was a beautiful rendition of the High Renaissance masterpiece, perfectly capturing the Master's command of space and perspective as well as his prowess in conveying human emotional communication.

As I stared at the painting, I remember thinking to myself: *How the fuck would my grandmother see it? Forget the fact that she's dead, even if she were* alive *how would she see it* inside *the casket? It's completely dark in there. If* I *hop in there right now and close the lid, I won't be able to see it. And once that lid's closed, no one* outside *the casket will be able to see it either. But even* that's *beside the point because once we bury her, the casket will be underground. No one'll be able to see the goddamned* coffin, *never mind the inside of the lid. So, in essence, that stupid painting will never be seen by anyone, living or dead.*

The Last Supper casket made no sense whatsoever. It was completely useless. Something you spend money on now to be used later by a dead person who won't be around to appreciate it anyway. In other words, *just like a legacy.*

Why Condemn Your Legacy Building?

Of all the fatuous things we humans do while we're alive, attempting to control what others think and know about us when we're dead is the very definition of insanity that Albert Einstein never said.*

You cannot enjoy your life in the here and now, embracing mediocrity and aiming for the middle, if you're hell-bent on

---

* While the saying "The definition of insanity is doing the same thing over and over again and expecting different results" is often credited to Albert Einstein, there is no evidence that Big Brains ever said it.

The quote has also been attributed to civil rights campaigner and feminist writer Rita Mae Brown in her 1983 book *Sudden Death.*

However, the quote may have actually originated in a 1981 Narcotics Anonymous pamphlet in the nominally different version "Insanity is repeating the same mistakes and expecting different results." (Thank you, cocaine!)

With all that said, the connection between repetition and insanity has been traced back to the 19th century. So, who really knows? You could go crazy trying to figure it out. Insanity is trying to find out who said the quote it and learning it's a different person over and over.

creating a transcendent life to impress other people when you're dead. *That's* the real definition of insanity—and you can attribute that quote to me.

Six Reasons Not to Build a Legacy

While there are myriad reasons to condemn your legacy building, the following six are vital for maintaining a standard of mediocrity necessary for a happy, successful, loving life.

1. Legacy building squanders precious time on a future you won't be around for.

There is an inherently paradoxical problem with legacies: they exist only when you're dead but you build them when you're alive. All screwy. This means you spend time, effort, and money on something you will never use, just like a gym membership.

Whether it's a collection of memorable and important events culled from a lifetime of work (think: filmmaker Renny Harlin's oeuvre) or a single, grandiose gesture made right before you kick the bucket (think: Lee Harvey Oswald), to build a lasting legacy such as the two I've cited, you'll have to set goals, take actions, face obstacles, work hard, fail hard, invest financially, and generally suck up a lot of time—all when you're still alive and could've been enjoying life relaxing and streaming Netflix (I *never* get tired of watching *Suits*. When I finish season 9, episode 10, I go right back to pilot and start all over again!).

Science has proven the results derived from an expenditure of your time, energy, and resources are far more beneficial to you when you're alive in the present rather than dead in the future. Therefore, anytime you feel a delusion of grandeur coming on and you find yourself designing your rich, phenomenal life without you in it, STOP! Watch a Renny Harlin movie (I highly recommend *Cutthroat Island* or *Exorcist: The Beginning*) or ponder where Lee Harvey's best planning got him. Let those legacy lessons really sink in. Then go create an adequate life you can enjoy when you're still around—not an extraordinary one you can't appreciate when you're gone.

2. Legacy building forces you to look at yourself... and it's not a pretty sight.

When constructing your legacy, you can detail your happiest times, commemorate your most important relationships, immortalize your greatest triumphs, or tell the truth. And therein rubs the lie: legacy building forces you to confront your mediocrity within the context of what you should've done, never did, aren't doing, and will never do.

This is why legacies sabotage your life of mediocrity. Mediocre plays great in life, not so great in death. For example, have you ever heard the following eulogy given at anyone's funeral?

Living a so-so life, [name of person honored] never reached above the ordinary, preferring instead to grasp for the adequate in everything they did. This acceptable life has born a vanilla legacy of satisfactory commitment to family and friends, middling innovations in their industry, uninspiring community outreach, and moderate charity work that made a pedestrian difference.

Actually, I wrote that to be sarcastic, but now that I read it, that's an impressively mediocre life—one I would personally be proud to call my own. But as a legacy? Ehhh, not so impressive.

A legacy is a highlights reel of your life. But what if your life didn't have any highlights—just midlights? Maybe you didn't change the world for the better with that new phone app that triangulates videos of your food with the restaurant's geographic location, pushing both to every social media platform in existence. That doesn't mean you had a bad life, just a mediocre legacy (and app). And as I've illustrated, mediocre legacies don't play well.

. . .

3. The future you may not play as well as the current you.

A legacy is a permanent record of who you *were*. So, it's imperative to remember that record does not change with the times; it's frozen in the social, political, ethical, and cultural perspectives of the period in which you forged it. Your legacy may paint you in a positive light now, but that light could turn dim, even dark, in the ensuing years.

Take, for example, Franklin Delano Roosevelt, the thirty-second president of these United States of America. He led the country through arguably the most dire epoch in its history: the Great Depression *and* World War II. This guy not only had to deal with all that *Grapes of Wrath* shit, but Mussolini, Hirohito, Stalin, and the king of all evil himself, Hitler! *And* he did it all from a wheelchair with fucking polio! FDR's legacy includes:

- The longest-serving American president—twelve years, two months, and twenty-three days.
- Successfully saw the country through the Great Depression.
- Reduced the nation's unemployment rate from 24 to 2 percent.
- Led the United States to victory in World War II.
- Created numerous institutions as part of the New Deal including the Public Works Administration (PWA) that created infrastructure that remains vital to this day.[1]
- Took part in the creation of the United Nations.
- Created the U.S. social security system.
- Established the minimum wage.
- Instituted the forty-hour workweek.
- Signed Executive Order 9066.
- Took action to prohibit discrimination in employment.
- Appointed the first woman ever to hold a U.S. presidential administration cabinet position (Frances Perkins, secretary of labor).

- Established the FDIC. Still used today, it insures bank deposits of up to $250,000 from banks that fail.
- Aided water pollution control.
- And much, much more!

Wow! What a legacy! This guy was the ultimate overachiever. And did I mention he did it all from a wheelchair with fucking polio?

So much of what FDR created and accomplished during his presidency over eighty years ago is still enjoyed and relied upon for a better life by hundreds of millions of United Statesians. I'm guessing you probably think this is one hell of a legacy. I'd bet you'd even say it's a legacy *you'd* be proud to have. And if you did, I'd say *au contraire*. That's because buried there in the fine print is something you likely overlooked; something that doesn't usually make it onto FDR's white-washed resume: *executive Order 9066*. Sounds innocuous enough, I know. Probably another amazing social program that continues to do good and solidify FDR's legacy, right? *Au contraire.*

Executive Order 9066 was the executive presidential order that Roosevelt signed authorizing the incarceration and relocation of 120,000 people of Japanese ancestry—sixty-two percent of whom were United States citizens—into internment camps.[2] A despicable action to be sure and a stain on any legacy. Just ask the San Francisco, California School Board who moved to strike his name from Roosevelt Middle School, having deemed him unworthy of the honor. Unfortunately, Roosevelt's name remains on the school due to a technicality: the school board could not ascertain whether the school was named after FDR or his fifth cousin, President Theodore "Teddy" Roosevelt (who himself has a tarnished legacy), or maybe some other Roosevelt.

FDR's legacy perfectly illustrates how the *current you* can fuck over the *future you*. You never know how history in the future will define your actions in the past. Changing times most often reframe your legacy for the worse—like with FDR. In retrospect, he would've been better off aiming for the middle because, in the end, he'll be remembered for having his name removed from a school in disgrace. Well, that is as soon as they confirm which Roosevelt it's actually named after.

4. If you have kids, they are your legacy—and there's not a damned thing you can do about it.

You can be the first person to discover new lands already inhabited by other people. You can buy immortality with the wing of a hospital bearing your name. You can even invent *both* peanut butter AND jelly in the same jar. But if you have kids, your legacy is already sealed. Fair or not, when you're long gone people will judge you by your children—how they turn out will be your *living* legacy. If your child was Martin Luther King Jr. then you, my friend, have an awesome legacy. On the other hand, Mr. and Mrs. Manson's selfless legacy of annual holiday canned food drives has been largely overshadowed by their son Charlie's work with young, impressionable hippies.

Since you have no idea who your child will grow up to be, saint or sinner, that's all the more reason in the universe *not* to exert yourself building a legacy—it will be irrelevant. If your kids somehow end up prominent, you can coast along on *their* spectacular legacy. But if they become a cannibal serial killer, or a brutal fascist dictator, or a member of an 80s cover band, you're fucked no matter what storybook bullshit you processed, packaged, and peddled about yourself.

And it doesn't even have to be anywhere near those extremes. If your kid just turns out to be a shitty parent and has their own fucked up kid, *that* will be your legacy: the parent of the fucked up kid who became a shitty parent with a fuck up kid. And boy, how do you fix *that*? You can't. So don't even try.

. . .

5. When it comes to a legacy, actions speak louder than exaggerations.

The biggest problem with a legacy is that most of it is *external* —it's what you attained, bought, or won. It says nothing of how happy you were, how [truly] successful you were, or how much you loved and were loved. A legacy won't tell anyone who the *real* you was.

Did you ever see that movie *It's a Wonderful Life*? It's the perineal Christmas movie that isn't really a Christmas movie about a guy who thinks his life is meaningless so he decides to off himself by jumping off a bridge that's like, fifteen feet above the water. Aside from the hope of a life-threatening sprained ankle, at least it was snowing so there was the chance he could've died from hypothermia in the freezing water because the short fall surely wouldn't have killed him.

Anyway, the dude's rescued by of all things a goofball angel-in-training. (Apparently, when we humans are about to take our own life, God sends in the B-team.) The goofball angel proves to the guy how meaningful his life actually is (was) by showing him an alternate reality where he never existed. Pretty clever conceit.

By seeing the positive impact he's had on everyone who knew him (including some Italians he bought a house for) our guy—*Spoiler alert!* —learns he really did have a wonderful life.

But the *real* message here (and the reason I wasted over half a page recounting one of the most well-known movies ever made) is that *our guy had already been working on his legacy just by living his life—he just didn't know it.* He had a profound effect on everyone in his life simply by living his rules, values, and beliefs —and the legacy thing took care of itself.

So, if you *must* build a legacy (and I still say you mustn't), then this option is hands-down the way to go. EZ and effortless, it's the aluminum standard for mediocre legacies.

. . .

Legacy Schmegacy

Rather than spending your time, effort, and money devising a life to leave behind, be the person you were going to fabricate *now* while you're still here so you can enjoy people enjoying you. Just live your life every day to its mediocre potential as if it were your last and leave the rest to the ages while you rest for ages.

PILLAR FIVE: TAKE A SHIT EVERY DAY

Strange and marvelous things will happen with constant regularity as you alter your life and begin living in harmony with the laws of the universe.

—Earl Nightingale

At my age, any constant regularity in my daily life is universally appreciated regardless of how harmonious or legally it happens.

—M. K. Jackson

Remember waaaaay back when, when you took your first SHIT in chapter 1? So much has transpired since then.

You've read and completed the entire book (*cough-cough*), designed your own *rules*, *values*, and *beliefs* to serve *your* life plan (not the agendas of other people and institutions), redefined *happiness*, *success*, and *love* (pretty much) to guarantee its attainment, and in recognition of all this, been awarded a Master of Mediocrity.

But it doesn't end there—and that's what pillar five is all about.

In chapter 1, the *Success and Happiness Indicator Test* was exploratory—a research tool to establish where you were before you began your journey into achieving happiness, success, and love through the unbridled power of mediocrity. Now that you've arrived, it's still important to continue your commitment to creating and maintaining a life that's good enough by taking a *daily* SHIT. Just refer back to chapter 1 for the test and how to take it. In time, you can even create your own questions to keep yourself aiming for the middle (but that's for some time down the line. Let's not overdo it by doing too much too soon… You gotta crawl before you can walk).

With each test score, remember to employ the three Rs—*react, reassess,* and *reset*—until you're consistently operating at the perfect 0-0-3 score.

And When All Else Fails, You Can Always Take AiM…

On those days when your streaming video backlog or napping schedule is just so overwhelming you don't even have time to take a SHIT, you can always use the acronym for **AiM**—*Achieve in Mediocrity* and that will keep you on track.

CONCLUSION

Life isn't about finding yourself. Life is about creating yourself.
   —George Bernard Shaw

*I found that the self I created still needed finding so I created this book
to do the looking.*
   —M.K. Jackson

C ongratulations! You made it all the way to the end! Well
   done you. And if you didn't read any of this book and just
jumped to the *Conclusion* as an EZ way to get the gist of the
whole thing, I'm impressed; you really aren't trying all that hard.
However, if you did arrive here by actually *reading* the whole
book, then I'm *very* impressed. Just reading *anything* is hella less
EZer—especially an entire goddamn book. Twenty-eight percent
of the respondents in a HuffPost/YouGov poll admitted to
reading *zero books* the previous year.[1] *Whoa—crack a fuckin' book
now and then, dudes!* That poll puts *you* in the top seventy-two
percent of folks who *do* read. Respect. But the *best* part? Now,
you don't have to read another book for a whole other year!

   I gotta admit, writing a book was a lot more difficult than I
thought it would be—especially one about not trying so hard.
Nevertheless, I sit in smug gratification with the way it turned

out: *finished*. Sure, it has some tipos, mispellings, dead-end think-ing, and contradictory logic. Not to mention missed humor opportunities and jokes that fell flatter than a pancake (as that joke just did).

But all that doesn't really matter in the long run because I *finished* the goddamned book, and I'm now a published author—*that* in and of itself is a success that makes me happy, and I love it!

Now that I've released this tome into the wild, my humble hope is that it will be counted amongst the most important volumes in the collective works of humanity, forever and profoundly affecting everyone who reads it—intellectually, emotionally, psychologically, and spiritually—making each and every one of its readers a happier, more successful, and loved individual than they were before they read it.

Or if people just think it's funny, that's cool too.

So, here's the deal: for the conclusion, rather than just regurgitating, reiterating, and recycling what I've already written (and what you've [maybe] already read), I'll distill it all down into these three takeaways:

The Three Key Takeaways from This Book

1. **Don't try so hard**—it's unnecessary, irrelevant, and exhausting.
2. **Stack the deck in your favor**—create your own definitions for your happiness, success, and love… you can better achieve that which *you* define.
3. **True happiness, success, and love are forged through the unbridled power of mediocrity**—see takeaway number 1 above.

4. **A life of realized adequacy is far more fulfilling than one of elusive excellence**—don't waste your life constantly failing to grab the brass cock ring. Eventually, the carousel stops turning and you'll be left holding your dick (or someone else's) in your hand.

Well, that was *four* takeaways and with that, I just violated takeaway number one (it's like I didn't even bother to read my own goddamn book).

Putting a Tale on It

I'll leave you with a story from my childhood, an instructive tale replete with heartbreak, triumph, and balsa wood. Decode its overly obvious metaphorical narrative and you will unravel the sweater of eternal happiness, success, and yes, even love…

When I was nine years old, I entered my Cub Scout pack's kite flying contest. The objective was straightforward: the kid with the highest-flying kite won.

For the big event, my dad and I designed and built a mammoth box kite of balsa wood and landscaping plastic. It was a showy piece to be sure. Bigger than a phone booth (if you remember those things), painted orange and purple (it was the 70s), and required speaker audio cable as kite string to avoid breaking.

When we arrived at the contest, the sheer size of the kite prompted "ooooos" and ahhhhs" from the other entrants. My competition even wanted their picture taken with my behemoth cellular wonder. By all accounts, my kite was a huge success.

Well, not by *all* accounts. There was one problem with it: the son of a bitch couldn't fly. Since neither my dad nor I were aerospace engineers, our design was flawed. The kite was too big (or maybe the air was too small). There was too much drag or not enough lift.

Maybe it needed more pixie dust... I dunno, I'm not an aerospace engineer. Even though there were some pretty gusty winds that day I couldn't get that colossus more than three feet in the air.

Now, making a box kite the size and weight of a refrigerator for a kite flying contest is like making a dildo the size and weight of a telephone pole for a dildo riding contest. Sure, it'll be a much-talked-about novelty piece and everyone will want to take their picture with it, but in the end (or front) it can't do what it's supposed to do. And so, you'll lose the contest because you can't fly a huge, heavy dildo.

A year later, when I was in fourth grade, my school held its own kite flying contest. And as sure as Cap'n Crunch has a sweet and golden ball sack with a crunch you'll love, I was primed and ready. I had learned my lesson. When it came time to select my kite for *this* contest, no showy lead balloons for me. This time I would strip it down to the simplest, smallest, lightest-weight, store-bought kite I could find.

I rode my bike to the local QuikStop convenience store (7-Eleven's illegitimate cousin twice removed) and purchased a plain ol' 69¢ Hi-Flier brand diamond kite with a Pegasus on it. It was so compact and lightweight that I carried it home on my bike (as opposed to that mammoth box kite inside of which I could've *parked* my bike).

On the afternoon of the contest, we all gathered on the playground with our kites. There were dozens of kids with every kite imaginable: delta kites, diamond kites, parafoil kites, sled kites, stunt kites, traction kites, and even cellular kites (AKA box kites). They were all made with everything from paper to plastic to nylon. Most kids piloted their kites with string off a wooden dowel. But some stepped it up with handled spools, twisting winders, and spinning reels. However, the real showoffs had the fanciest of all string management systems: the *Hi-Flier Professional Spinwinder**—a large, red plastic spindle that spooled and

---

* As a 10-year-old boy, seeing the "professional" Spinwinder I couldn't believe

unspooled kite string via a yellow wooden ball knob at the end of a metal crank, done so with the precision and execution of a... *professional.*

Regardless of all that nonsense, I kept my pledge to use a rudimentary kite of the simplest construction with a basic string rig wound around a cardboard tube. Manifest and mediocre.

When it was time for the competition to commence, Mrs. Gausen, the school principal, explained the straightforward rules: after fifteen minutes, the highest-flying kite wins. And with that, Mrs. Gausen clicked her stopwatch and it was *game on!*

Every contestant immediately and simultaneously launched their kite—every contestant that is but me. Unaware of the contest's rigid time frame I had not previously assembled my kite, giving all the other kite jockeys the jump on me. At that moment, I figured it was over for me. My little, soon-to-be-arterial-plaque-blocked heart dropped into my stomach. *I should've assembled my kite before I got to school!* Now there was no way I'd ever catch up to everyone else. I was going to lose my *second* kite flying contest. *Nice goin', Schleprock.*

There are instances in life that, when they happen, look to be the worst possible outcome at the worst possible moment but are, in fact, blessings in disguise. We've all experienced them, it's just that we rarely recognize them at the time. As despondent as I was didn't realize this was one of those times, for my late launch would prove to be most fortuitous.

Several frantic minutes later I finally finished building my kite and looked to the sky. There, above the playground, was a congested low ceiling of immobilized kites. Every kite in the contest took off at the same time so they had all become entangled while fighting for the same airspace. Because I was so late to the party, I was unable to launch my kite into that airborne

---

that somewhere in this world there were PROFESSIONAL kite flyers—people (kids???) who were actually PAID to fly kites as their JOB! But the very existence of this state-of-the-art piece of elite equipment was *proof* of it!

mess. I was providentially spared the kite traffic jam. And that's when it dawned on me…

Because all the kites were stuck in a tangled mess, *they* too were unable to move anywhere—*including up*. That was as high as they were gonna go—and it wasn't very high. Flying my kite higher than that would be a snap—in an open area.

I looked away from the playground and over to the kickball field. *It was completely empty*. Not one kite flyer in the entire area. The rules mandated how much *time* we had to fly our kite but not *where* we could fly it. So, I hot-tailed my ass (and kite) over to the field. Away from the cluster dance of kites on the playground, I had unlimited sky all to myself. I set sail and with the clear flight path, my kite took off like a rocket and soared into the stratosphere. Man, I couldn't let the sting out fast enough. My kite climbed higher and higher.

By the time the fifteen minutes were up, I was pretty sure my kite had pierced the mesosphere. Mrs. Gausen spotted my cheap little store-bought kite dancing all alone way the hell up there dodging meteors and challenging satellites. She waved her arm at me from across the field, pointed up at my kite, and declared me the winner. *I was better than everyone else and I had proved it!*

It took me quite a while to pull my kite in from outer space. Meanwhile, all those idiot kids were still trying to unfangle (unfuck and un-tangle) their kites from the snarled mess they made for themselves by not being as smart as me.

As the winner of the contest, I was given first choice among three prizes—a pencil case, a kite, and the one I selected: *a horse figurine* (of all things)—you know, like a Pegasus. I remember thinking it wasn't necessarily the *best* prize, but it was the most apposite to the circumstances. It's as if the whole thing was preordained. Ain't that a kick in the head?

Like the ending of the movie *Psycho*, this is where I explain everything to you so the narrative makes sense. I tell you that the point of this story is since I was the smartest kid in my entire school, I was better than everyone else and that's why I won the prize. Unfortunately, while true, this interpretation has nothing at all to do with any of the theories proposed in this book.

Could be the meaning of the story is that thinking outside the box kite and not following all the sheeple is the key to winning in life. Yeah, that's good… but it doesn't really have anything to do with the premise of this book either.

But the more I think about it, I guess maybe the point of the story is just because you put a lot of work and resources into something (big box kites or huge dildos) it doesn't necessarily mean you'll get the best results. Sometimes not trying so hard and employing the most mediocre option (store-bought kites or average-sized dildos) can yield the best outcome—or at least one that's good enough.

Yeah, I'd say that interpretation of the story is closest to what this book is all about, so I'll just stop there and go with that.

Unless, of course, you have a better one.

ACKNOWLEDGMENTS

This book has enjoyed far more support than deserved or required. For those implicated, I offer my profound gratitude.

Aim for the Middle was birthed in the Legacy Launch Pad Write Launch Group. Anna David and the generous writers in the group including Barbara, Heidi, Kimberly, Shuna, Conrad, and Tim for their feedback and encouragement.

My support sphere of friends including, Laurel, Luis, Noelle, Diane, and my dearly departed cat William (who kept me company during all those hours of writing).

The enchanted Caffe Trieste with its wonderful baristas, namely William (who kept me filled and fueled with cappuccino grandes).

And my mother and father who unwaveringly supported my creative pursuits from my cradle to their graves. It all led to this. I'll bet they're sorry now.

NOTES

PREFACE

1. https://news.gallup.com/poll/1720/work-work-place.aspx
2. https://www.norc.org/PDFs/COVID%20Response%20Tracking%20Study/NSF_COVID_Topline.pdf
3. https://www.prnewswire.com/news-releases/united-states-self-improvement-products-and-services-market-report-2019-examination-of-the-11-billion-industry-300938743.html.

2. YOUR SUCCESSFUL, HAPPY, LOVING LIFE (PART 1)

1. https://divorce.com/blog/divorce-statistics/
2. https://www.businessinsider.com/why-people-get-divorced-2019-1

4. EPIPHANY ONE: I'M TRYING TOO HARD

1. https://www.forbes.com/sites/adigaskell/2018/04/02/what-role-does-luck-play-in-success/?sh=4f4d391c357d

8. WHEN LIFE GIVES YOU LEMONS, MAKE WHISKEY SOURS

1. Meyer, Nicholas (dir), *Star Trek II: The Wrath of Khan*, United States, Paramount Pictures, 1982, 35mm film, 2.39:1.

EPIPHANY THREE: DON'T PUT THE SUCCESS CART BEFORE THE HAPPINESS HORSE

1. https://www.merriam-webster.com/dictionary/natural%20order
2. https://www.forbes.com/sites/nickbennett1/2018/11/18/the-secret-of-success-is-it-happiness/?sh=1264a3236aa9
3. https://www.inc.com/jeff-haden/a-surprising-truth-about-misunderstood-relationship-between-happiness-success.html
4. https://www.fastcompany.com/90731186/which-comes-first-happiness-or-success

9. MEDIOCRE JOKER

1. https://www.merriam-webster.com/dictionary/mediocre
2. Oxford English Dictionary

3. https://www.dictionary.com/browse/alternative
4. https://www.dictionary.com/browse/moderate
5. https://web.archive.org/web/20170617103245/https://www.edge.org/q2011/q11_12.html#myerspz
6. Credit Suisse Research Institute Global Wealth Report 2019 (page 9)
7. https://www.boxofficemojo.com/year/?sort=year&ref_=bo_yl__resort#table
8. Fifteen different films received awards counting Best Live Action Short, Best Documentary Short, and Best Animated Short. However, those three films were not included among those in the 439 releases cited by Box Office Mojo.
9. https://courses.lumenlearning.com/suny-ushistory2os2xmaster/chapter/united-states-population-chart/
10. http://www.hsbaseballweb.com/probability.htm
11. https://www.yourswimlog.com/what-are-my-chances-of-going-to-the-olympics/
12. https://www.yourswimlog.com/what-are-my-chances-of-going-to-the-olympics/

10. THE FIVE OR SIX DESTRUCTIVE BELIEFS PREVENTING YOU FROM ACHIEVING HAPPINESS, SUCCESS, AND LOVE

1. https://work.chron.com/statistics-people-getting-famous-acting-23946.html
2. New Living Translation.
3. King James Version. Sorta paraphrased, but you get the point.

12. BUT ENOUGH ABOUT YOU—WHAT DO YOU THINK OF YOU?

1. https://www.mayoclinic.org/diseases-conditions/narcissistic-personality-disorder/symptoms-causes/syc-20366662
2. https://dictionary.apa.org/self-confidence
3. https://www.yourdictionary.com/self-love

13. A HOW-TO GUIDE TO SELF-LOVE

1. https://www.mayoclinic.org/healthy-lifestyle/fitness/expert-answers/exercise/faq-20057916
2. https://www.psychologytoday.com/intl/blog/the-resilient-brain/201704/restorative-sleep-is-vital-brain-health
3. https://vitalrecord.tamhsc.edu/6-weird-body-facts/
4. https://www.psychologytoday.com/us/blog/what-mentally-strong-people-dont-do/201504/7-scientifically-proven-benefits-gratitude

17. STEP 3: ALIGN YOUR RULES, VALUES, AND BELIEFS

1. https://www.merriam-webster.com/dictionary/author
2. https://dictionary.cambridge.org/us/dictionary/english/author
3. https://www.dictionary.com/browse/author

18. STEP 4: REDEFINE YOUR DEFINITIONS OF HAPPINESS, SUCCESS, AND LOVE

1. https://www.the-numbers.com/movie/Rocky#tab=summary. For those less math inclined (as myself), $22,500% of its $1 million budget = $225 million worldwide return.
2. https://www.zippia.com/answers/what-percentage-of-the-worlds-adult-population-are-millionaires/
3. https://www.nbcnews.com/politics/politics-news/americans-are-unhappiest-they-ve-been-50-years-poll-finds-n1231153
4. https://divorce.com/blog/divorce-statistics/#:~:text=The%20United%20States%20has%20the,dropped%20from%202009%20to%202019

PILLAR ONE: LOWER YOUR EXPECTATIONS

1. https://www.rottentomatoes.com/franchise/indiana_jones
2. https://www.ign.com/articles/2017/08/02/steven-spielberg-thinks-temple-of-doom-is-the-worst-indiana-jones-movie
3. https://www.boxofficemojo.com/title/tt0087469/?ref_=bo_se_r_1
4. Lyric from Enjoli perfume commercial (1979), based on I'm A Woman (1962) written by Jerry Leiber & Mike Stoller.

PILLAR TWO: EMBRACE COMPLACINCY

1. https://dictionary.cambridge.org/us/dictionary/english/complacency

PILLAR THREE: FOR GOD'S SAKE, STOP SETTING GOALS

1. https://www.inc.com/marcel-schwantes/science-says-only-8-percent-of-people-actually-achieve-their-goals-here-are-7-things-they-do-differently.html

PILLAR FOUR: CONDEMN YOUR LEGACY BUILDING

1. https://en.wikipedia.org/wiki/Public_Works_Administration
2. https://en.wikipedia.org/wiki/Internment_of_Japanese_Americans

CONCLUSION

1. https://www.huffpost.com/entry/american-read-book-poll_n_4045937

ERRATA

Before this book went to press, I did take the time to proofread it. While I found several errors and corrected them, I am under no illusion that many also slipped by me—especially commas. Goddamn commas. I have a history of over-commalizing. I also under-commalize. How's that even possible? I have no idea, but I do it.

I'm also sure I missed spelling errors and missing words.

I am not, however, going to count jokes that fell flat (and nor should you).

I guess I probably should've given the manuscript another proofing (or at least had someone else do it). But to be honest, I SO wanted to just finish this damn book, I, literally, could not spend one more minute working on it (*did you catch that? I over-commalized again—it's like a disorder I have*).

Regarding any errors I missed that you may have discovered, my apologies. But frankly, spending any more time working on this book would've been counter to its central thesis.

However, should you be amenable to citing any errata you spotted, I've included a chart to record your discoveries:

Your Errata Discoveries

Page	Paragraph	As written	Correction

ABOUT THE AUTHOR

The only known photograph of the author (seen on the right) taken back when it all started to go wrong. Original 1970s Polaroid black and white snapshot.

M.K. Jackson has authored countless resumes, several essays, and numerous unfinished books including *Baby's First Exorcism*, *Testicular Manslaughter*, and *100 Years of Mold and Mildew*.

Jackson has more degrees than a thermometer, all of them overstated, underearned, and equally useless: a Bachelor of Arts (can't get a job with it, can't teach with it), a Master of Fine Arts (can't get a job with it but can teach with it), and a Doctor of Divinity (can't teach with it but can officiate weddings with it).

The author currently resigns in Los Angeles, California, with his childhood friend, a large, anthropomorphic white rabbit.

He's available for weddings (Jackson, not the rabbit).

CONNECT

If, for some reason, you need to contact me, **PLEASE DO NOT COME TO MY HOUSE.** Instead, use the World Wide Web's electronic mail system:

mkjacksonwriter@gmail.com

Prefer to kick it in the old school with a letter or postcard? Commission the United States Postal Service:

M.K. Jackson
P.O. Box 421572
Los Angeles, CA 90042

———

I can also be contacted via Ouija Board. If I do not respond immediately, I'm probably in another dimension. Please continue to hold and I should materialize shortly.

———

Websites

mkjackson.com

As if the innernet wasn't fun enough already, **mkjackson.com** is a cyber wonderland of delicious bite-sized treats all low in calories and all good for you.

aimforthemiddlebook.com

The official website for this book. You'll find trips and ticks for leading a life of abundant mediocrity, special offers on *Aim for the Middle* gear, and social media cards to spread the word on living life to its most adequate.

Subscribe to my official electronic newsletter. A brief but impactful read to start off the end of your week with a slang. Chockablock with news and reviews, updates and excuses, insights and delights, it's like having me roaming around in your inbox—but with permission this time.

Signup for the M.K. Jackson eNewsletter

————

Check out all the other pies I have my fingers in…
MySpace: **mkjackson**
Instagram: **mkjacksonwriter**
X (Twitter): **mkjacksonwriter**
Facebook: **mkjacksonwriter**
Medium: **mkjackson.medium.com**

————

If you have a beef with this book please don't drag me into it. Instead, contact my publisher, Purple Prose Publishing LLC. They're trained to handle that sort of thing.

purpleprosepublishing.com